The Ne

G000274567

About the Book

For anyone attendir
meeting for the first ti....
of the TV, the spectacle will probably present a bewildering
and ever-moving variety of sights and sounds. *The New
Observer's Book of Athletics* aims to clarify this spectacle in a
lively and interesting way, and in so doing functions as an
excellent introduction to the whole exciting world of athletics.

After a short description of the historical development and
modern organization of the sport worldwide, there is a
description in words and pictures of the athletics stadium: its
layout, equipment, the track officials, and what the well-
dressed athlete should look like. Then each event is high-
lighted – laying special emphasis not just on what happens
but why it happens – and both major established and up-and-
coming world personalities for each event are profiled. The
book rounds off with an important and informative records
section.

First published in Olympics year, *The New Observer's Book
of Athletics* is completely international in scope. Illustrated
with numerous specially commissioned drawings by one of
Britain's top sports illustrators, and with many fine photographs, this visually exciting book succeeds magnificently in
presenting the athletics scene in a way never attempted
before.

About the Author

Steve Brennan not only writes about athletics but is also an
active participator and has competed as a cross country and
middle distance runner for Thames Valley Harriers – one of
Britain's top clubs. He has been a feature writer and reporter
for some time now, and has contributed to all of Britain's most
popular athletics periodicals, including *Athletics Monthly,
Athletes World, Athletics Weekly* and *Marathon and Distance
Runner. The New Observer's Book of Athletics* is his first full-
length book.

The New Observer's Book of
Athletics

Steve Brennan

with drawings by
Geoff Harrold

Frederick Warne

First published 1984 by Frederick Warne (Publishers) Ltd,
London

© 1984 Frederick Warne (Publishers) Ltd

Acknowledgements: The author would like to thank Stan
Greenberg and Cliff Temple for their generous help in
producing this book. The author and publishers would like
to thank Mark Shearman for supplying all the photographs
in the book, with the exception of that on page 21, which
was supplied by All-Sport Photographic Ltd.

ISBN 0 7232 1677 0

Printed and bound in Great Britain by
William Clowes Limited, Beccles and London

CONTENTS

INTRODUCTION

Athletics is a varied and exciting sport, but unless the spectator has a basic knowledge and understanding of the different aspects of the competition, and is familiar with the names and achievements of some of the more outstanding athletes, then even the most absorbing and eventful of track or field contests may be totally bewildering. The purpose of *The New Observer's Book of Athletics* is to clarify the spectacle of an action-packed athletics meeting in a lively and interesting way, and in so doing enable the reader to appreciate and enjoy the sport to the full.

Few other sports can boast as long and eventful a history as that of athletics—and this fascinating story is outlined in the first part of this book. Filling in the all-important background to the athletics competition itself, there are sections dealing with the sport's complex organization, the layout of the modern athletics stadium, the sophisticated equipment found within it, and the many officials who help to ensure the smooth running of national and international competitions.

The major section of the book is dedicated to the numerous and diverse events which go to make up the various branches of the sport. Within these pages, in addition to the technical aspects of each event, precise skills and competition tactics are explained and an idea of what constitutes a meaningful performance—in terms of time or measurement—is given. Throughout this and the comprehensive Records section that rounds off the book, metric measurements predominate over their imperial equivalents. Many English-speaking nations, notably the USA, have been slow to introduce metrication, but if the athletics enthusiast is to gain a full appreciation of performances, particularly in the field events, he or she will need to become completely familiar with this virtually universal method of measurement.

Immediately following the description of each particular event is a selection of concise yet informative biographies of just some of the event's outstanding personalities – featuring both established stars and those to look out for in the future.

GLOSSARY OF ATHLETICS TERMS

Aerobic running   Running at a pace at which the athlete can inhale sufficient oxygen to replenish that being burned up by the muscles. Conversely, **anaerobic running** involves a rate of activity that burns up oxygen faster than the athlete can replenish it, as in sprint races.

Altitude training   Training conducted at specially sited high altitude training venues. This is of particular value to middle and long distance runners, for the thin air at high altitude causes an increase in the oxygen-carrying capacity of the blood, thereby improving respiration and consequently enhancing athletic performance in the richer atmosphere at sea level.

Anchor leg   The final leg, or stage, of a relay race on the track, road or country—often reserved for the fastest member of each team.

Approach run   Field athlete's run-up preceding a jump or throw in any of the four jumping events and the javelin.

Automatic timing   Fully automatic electronic timing.

Backstraight   *See* Straight.

Baton   The hollow aluminium or plastic cylinder which is passed from one runner to another during a track relay race.

Bell lap (or **gun lap**)   The final lap of a middle or long distance track race, the start of which is signalled by the ringing of a bell or, as in the USA, the firing of a gun.

Break (from lanes)   The point at which the runners in the outside lanes cut into the inside lane of the track after a staggered start, during a race such as an 800 metres or 4 × 400 metres relay.

Cage   A tall metal frame supporting a heavy hemp net that partially surrounds the throwing circles for the hammer and discus events, designed to prevent implements from flying in the direction of spectators if released accidentally.

Callisthenics   Stretching and suppling exercises used by sprinters, hurdlers, jumpers and throwers as part of the warm up routine to improve mobility for competition.

Change down   The transition, during a 400 metres hurdles race, from one stride pattern to another involving a greater

8

number of strides between each of the hurdles.

Check marks Indicators such as coloured tape or even spare shoes placed on or alongside the runway in the jumping events to help the athlete judge his run up more accurately.

Crouch start The starting position used by sprinters and hurdlers in which the athlete adopts a bent leg position, with the foot of one leg and both the knee and foot of the other leg in contact with the track.

Dash An American term referring to the shorter sprints of 100 metres or less.

Dead heat A race finish in which two or more athletes reach the finish line at exactly the same instant—a rare occurrence but most likely in sprint events.

Dip finish A lunging dive executed just before the finish line, particularly by sprinters and hurdlers, to gain vital inches over opponents.

Doping The use of drugs to enhance athletic performance artificially.

False start A false start is committed when an athlete moves or begins to run before the starter's gun is fired to signal the commencement of a race.

Fartlek A form of training, of Swedish origin, for middle and long distance runners in which the athlete alternates periods of fast and slow running during a training run, preferably in open country.

Fastest losers Track athletes who have qualified for later rounds or finals of their events by achieving one of the fastest times in the heats, outside of an actual qualifying placing in a particular heat.

Finishing 'kick' A runner's sprint finish over the last lap, or part of the last lap, of a middle or long distance race.

'Flyer' An exceptionally fast start in a sprint race resulting either from the athlete marginally anticipating the start without detection or due to his unusually sharp reactions.

Gun lap *See* Bell lap.

Hamstring injury Common athletics injury, especially in sprinters and hurdlers, in which the tendon located behind the knee (hamstring) is wrenched or even torn, usually when the athlete is running at full speed.

Hare (or **rabbit**) An athlete who is entered in a middle or long distance track race, not with the intention of winning but specifically to set a fast pace in the early stages of the race, in order to lay the foundations for a record attempt or at least a fast overall time by the other runners in the field.

Heat   Track race serving as a preliminary elimination round before a final in a track and field meeting.

'Hitting the wall'   A popular phrase used to describe the point during a long distance running event, such as a marathon, when a runner experiences a sudden and often dramatic increase in fatigue as his body begins to utilize its fat reserves for energy after the more readily available carbohydrate energy has become depleted.

Homestraight   *See* Straight.

Infield   The area of an athletics arena situated inside the main track which accommodates all of the throwing event facilities and sectors plus many, if not all, of the jumping event facilities.

Jump-off   A contest in which tying athletes at the end of a high jump or pole vault competition attempt progressively higher or lower heights until the tie is resolved deciding the winner.

Junior   General term applying to young male or female athletes still in their teens.

Kick   *See* Finishing 'kick'.

Lane draw   The sequence of competitors' starting positions in track races run in lanes, determined randomly by officials or perhaps by computer at major international meetings.

Leading leg   In the steeplechase and hurdles events, the athlete's leading leg is the one which precedes his torso in clearing the obstacles, whereas the **trailing leg**, as the name suggests, trails the rest of the body over the barriers.

'Lifting'   The illegal practice in race walking of breaking continuous contact with the ground by raising the rearmost foot clear of the ground fractionally before the foremost foot has regained contact.

Long distance running   Track, road or cross-country events of at least 5000 metres (3 miles 188 yards) in length can be considered as long distance running.

Medals   In all types of athletics competition successful athletes are invariably awarded medals. The most valued medals are the gold, silver and bronze varieties awarded for first, second and third places, respectively, at major international track and field championships and competitions.

Meeting (or **meet**)   Gathering of athletes competing in a programme of athletics events held over one or several days.

Middle distance running   All running events from 800 metres to 3000 metres, or even 2 miles, come within the scope of middle distance running.

Multi-events   Those track and field competitions, contested both by men and women, that are a combination of several running, jumping and throwing events held usually over two days, i.e. the decathlon and heptathlon.

No-jump/no-throw   A jump or throw in any of the standard field events which does not satisfy the rules and regulations pertaining to that particular event and does not, therefore, count in the competition.

Official   Individual who performs various duties relating to the organization and general running of all types of athletics competition.

Oxygen debt   The amount of oxygen that an athlete must absorb via respiration, following all-out effort, to replenish that utilized by the muscles during the effort.

Pacemaker   A runner who leads the rest of the field during a middle or long distance race.

Permit meetings   International invitation athletics meetings for which an official permit has been granted by the world athletics governing body, the IAAF. Considered of greater international significance that other invitation meetings, these permit meetings are more closely controlled and directly sanctioned by the IAAF.

Personal best   An individual athlete's best performance in a particular athletics event throughout his/her athletics career.

Photo finish   The finish of a track race for which a photograph is required to determine the final placings where several competitors have crossed the finish line almost simultaneously, making it impossible to judge the finish accurately with the naked eye alone.

Plant   The action of inserting the far end of the vaulting pole into the vaulting box beneath the uprights, immediately before the pole vaulter takes off at the end of his run-up.

Qualifying standards   For all major international track and field celebrations, athletes wishing to compete are expected to achieve certain qualifying standards in their chosen events within a specified period prior to the competition, before they can be considered to represent their national teams.

Quartering wind   The wind direction most helpful to the discus thrower, i.e. blowing towards the front of the throwing circle from an angle, rather than head-on.

Relay race   Track, road or cross-country race between teams of athletes in which each individual team member runs one stage, or leg, of the total race distance.

Round   All athletics field event competitions comprise several rounds. In the horizontal jumps and throws a round consists of a series of jumps or throws, one for each and every competitor contesting the event, regardless of whether the attempt is valid or not.

Scoring tables   Official tables used to ascribe points values to specific performances in the track and field events which go to make up the multi-events.

Scratch line (or **Start line**)   The white line drawn across the width of the track, or across each individual lane, immediately behind which the athlete takes up his starting position to begin a race. In the field events the foul line at the end of the javelin runway is also referred to as a scratch line.

Sector   The designated area of the stadium infield within which implements used in the throwing events must land.

Splits   Times recorded at intermediate points during a race of 400 metres or longer to give an indication of whether the overall pace is fast or slow.

Sprints   Track events, up to and including 400 metres, run at full speed for the entire race distance.

Staggered start   Start of a race run in lanes in which the competitors in the outer lanes start from scratch lines several metres ahead of those in the lanes inside them, to counteract the extra distance involved in running wide round a bend.

Stopboard   A curved piece of wood 10 cm (4 in) thick affixed to the front of the shot put circle. When throwing, the shot putter braces his foot against the stopboard to avoid falling forwards out of the circle.

Straight (or **straightaway**)   Long, straight section of the standard track adjoining the bends. The straight situated nearest the main stand is termed the homestraight and the other, the backstraight.

Stride pattern   The calculated number of strides that a hurdler must take between the obstacles to arrive at the correct take-off point, and on the correct take-off leg, at each obstacle.

Surging   A tactic employed in long distance running events in which an athlete will alternately increase and decrease the race pace while in the lead, in order to tire his rivals by disrupting their running rhythm.

Synthetic track   A general term used to describe all types of artificial surface tracks.

Take-off leg   Applied to the jumping and hurdles events, this is the leg that produces the propulsion to clear either the bar or the hurdle, or to achieve horizontal jumping distance at the moment of take-off.

Takeover zones   Zones marked in each lane of a standard 400 metres track within which relay baton changeovers must be executed.

Tape   Band or cord stretched across the track or race finish, at about waist height above the finish line, to help the competitors judge the exact finishing point of the race.

Trailing leg   *See* Leading leg.

Trial events   Specially staged track and field events, the results of which assist athletics team selectors to determine the best of the athletes available to represent teams competing usually in major competition.

Tying up   A condition sometimes experienced by runners during the latter stages of the longer sprint events, where lactic acid builds up in the leg muscles to such an extent that their function becomes temporarily impaired causing the athlete to slow dramatically towards the finish of the race.

Veteran   Athlete still competing at the age of 40 or over in the case of a male or 35 and over in the case of a female.

Warming up, warming down   Pre- and post-competition exercises, the former preparing muscles for strenuous competitive activity and the latter helping to prevent muscles stiffening up after such activity.

Wind reading   Wind velocity measurement that has a bearing on performances in the sprints and horizontal jumps, especially where records are concerned.

Wind-up   A phase of the hammer thrower's technique in which the athlete rotates in the throwing circle, swinging the hammer around in a wide arc at an ever increasing speed.

ATHLETICS IN ANCIENT GREECE AND ROME

There is historical evidence of organized foot races in Egypt as long ago as 3800 BC but athletics in a form resembling the running, jumping and throwing events of the modern-day sport was first practised by the ancient Greeks as part of their Olympic Games celebrations, which are thought to have started around the thirteenth century BC. The ancient Olympic Games of 776 BC were the first for which precise records were kept and the first named Olympic champion was one Coroibos of Elis, who won a sprint race of approximately 170 m (558 ft) in length.

Staged every fourth year at the sacred site of Olympia in western Peloponnesus, the ancient Olympic Games developed into a five-day religious festival incorporating sporting events on the second, third and fourth days. The most popular of the Olympic athletics events was the pentathlon, held on the second day along with the chariot races. Remarkably like the modern multi-events, the ancient Greek pentathlon consisted of discus throwing, long jumping, javelin throwing, sprinting and wrestling. Throwing the discus (made of stone or cast metal and weighing up to 6.8 kg (15 lb) was judged more on aesthetic style than throwing distance, whilst the javelin thrower used a leather thong, attached to the shaft, when throwing to impart greater velocity and stability to the implement in flight, for accuracy was an important aspect of this ancient event. The long jump competitors were permitted to use hand-held weights (*halteres*) when jumping which helped to propel the jumper further if swung correctly. By this method a Spartan athlete named Chionis is reported to have jumped 7.05 m (23 ft 1½ in) at the Games of 656 BC.

Foot races, run not on a circular track but between posts situated approximately 190 m (623 ft) apart at either end of the stadium field, were held on the third day. There was a long distance race of 24 *stades* (stadium lengths) which covered approximately 4.5 km (2¾ miles), and two sprint races of 1 and 2 *stades*, respectively, the former being very much the 'blue riband' event. There was also a race for shield-carrying foot soldiers on the fourth day.

Athletes in the ancient Olympic Games often competed naked.

At first women were strictly forbidden even to watch the Olympic Games, although they did participate in their own four-yearly Heraea Games, named after Hera the wife of Zeus.

So great was the religious significance and prestige attached to an Olympic victory that every major Greek city built elaborate sports facilities and organized sports training schools to foster potential Olympic champions. During the sixth century BC, paid professional Olympic athletes came on the scene and around 50 BC the first association of professional athletes was formed.

When Greece became part of the Roman Empire in the second century BC the Romans preserved the Olympic Games, mainly out of a sense of nostalgia, for they did not share the Greeks' religious beliefs or their love of sport. However, under Roman rule the Olympic Games gradually lost their status, firstly through the inclusion of foreign competitors from Rome, Africa and Asia, when previously only athletes of pure Greek blood qualified to compete, and then with events such as the staging of rival 'Olympic Games' in the non-Olympic year of AD 67 by the Roman emperor Nero, who himself competed in and was allowed to win the chariot race.

Finally, in AD 394, the year after the 293rd Olympic celebration, Emperor Theodosius ended the Olympic Games by decree to bring to a close a tradition which had spanned almost 18 centuries.

THE AMATEUR ATHLETIC ASSOCIATION

Founded in 1880, the Amateur Athletic Association (known as the AAA) is primarily responsible for the organization and general running of men's amateur athletics in England and Wales, and is the sport's oldest national governing body, boasting well over 1,000 member athletics clubs. During that first year of existence the AAA inaugurated its own annual athletics meeting, the AAA Championships, which were open to British and overseas athletes right from the early days and were so well organized that before the modern Olympic Games became fully established, the meeting was looked upon as the unofficial World Championships. Held at several London venues over the years, the AAA Championships began life at the Lillie Bridge ground but since 1970 have been staged at the Crystal Palace National Sports Centre in London.

As athletics' first national governing body the AAA was quick to set a number of trends in many areas of the sport which have greatly influenced the subsequent development of both national and international athletics, and which still have a worldwide influence today. In time for the first Championships, the AAA was responsible for drawing up a list of 16 Rules for Competition, which determined factors such as the size, shape and weight of throwing implements. These same rules were adopted for the first modern Olympic Games celebration in 1896 and although there are now well over 100 AAA Rules for Competition, the majority of the original 16 still apply. The AAA was also the first official governing body to produce a list of ratified national athletics records, which was published on 16 April 1887. Today the AAA still has responsibility for ratifying AAA National Records (see pp. 30–33).

Before the AAA came on the scene the greatest problem in English athletics was that of class distinction. The wealthy upper classes formed their own exclusive athletics clubs which discriminated against working-class athletes, some of whom were paid professional runners. The upper-class athletes, or 'gentleman amateurs' as they liked to be known, were, however, mainly responsible for introducing constructive organization into amateur athletics, firstly through university bodies such as Oxford University's Exeter College Athletics Club, formed in 1850 and currently the oldest surviving club in the world. The Amateur Athletics Club, a London-based organization, was set up in 1866 to try to gain control of English athletics but despite the efforts of the AAC's most innovative committee member, John Graham Chambers, strong opposition from the influential London Athletics Club and organizations from the North and Midlands effectively prevented the proposed take-over.

It was left to three young Oxford University men, namely Clement N. Jackson, a tutor at Hertford College, and two students connected with the University Athletics Club, Bernard R. Wise and Montague Shearman, to settle the differences between the main contenders and bring them all together for the historic meeting at the Randolph Hotel, Oxford, on 24 April 1880, at which the AAA was born. During the meeting it was agreed that the Objects of the Association were:

1. To improve management of athletics meetings and promote uniformity of rules governing those meetings and the sport in general.
2. To repress abuse of the sport of athletics.
3. To hold an annual championship meeting.

Perhaps more important, the 28 delegates present finally agreed on the currently accepted definition of an 'amateur' athlete. As originally applied to athletics the word 'amateur' referred to a spectator or athletics fan, rather than to a competitor, but towards the mid-eighteenth century the term was used more and more by athletes from the upper classes to distinguish them from their working-class brothers, regardless of the fact that not all athletes from the lower classes were professionals. With the words 'mechanic, artisan and labourer'—which had specifically debarred working-class participation in amateur competition—being deleted from the previously accepted definition, the biggest stumbling-block in the development of English athletics was removed and the sport was at last opened to anyone, irrrespective of class, who wanted to compete for reasons other than financial gain.

THE IAAF

As international athletics began to take off at the beginning of the twentieth century, headed by the increasingly popular Olympic Games, there clearly became a need for a supreme governing body to provide worldwide control and guidance for the sport. To this end a congress was held in Stockholm on 17 July 1912, under the chairmanship of Swedish steel magnate J. Sigfrid Edström. The meeting was attended by representatives from 17 countries, including the United Kingdom and the United States, and the foundations for what has since become the largest international sports authority in the world, the International Amateur Athletic Federation, were laid. The Federation's main priorities in those days were to draft and implement rules and regulations for international competition; to formulate an internationally acceptable amateur definition; and officially to recognize athletics world records.

At the IAAF's second Congress in Berlin in 1913 the first Constitution was accepted and Edström was elected as the first Federation President. The first Technical Rules were introduced at the 1914 Congress in Lyon and in the same year a list of inaugural world records was published, incorporating a total of 83 men's records for running, hurdling, relays and walking, plus 12 field event records including the decathlon. The IAAF Congress is now held biennially, during each Olympic year and on the even years in between. The IAAF Council meets once per year.

Today the IAAF is an influential body with the power to discipline its members, and individual athletes where necessary, and under whose rules all international competition in member countries is conducted. In 1921 the IAAF became involved in assisting the International Olympic Committee to organize and stage the athletics programme for the most prestigious of sports celebrations, the Olympic Games; a duty which remains to this day one of the Federation's most important functions.

The rapid spread of international athletics on every continent has necessitated the formation of six distinct Continental Associations within the IAAF (representing

Africa, Asia, Europe, North and Central America, Oceania and South America), which now control international competition in their regions. A delegate from each of the six Associations sits on the IAAF Council to ensure worldwide representation. In addition, the sheer complexity of international athletics has made it necessary for the IAAF to allocate certain responsibilities to a number of committees within its organization. A technical committee deals with the rules of competition; there is a women's committee, a cross-country and road running committee, a walking committee and, most recently, a committee concerned with sports-related medical problems.

Still a major feature of the IAAF's responsibilities is the acceptance or rejection of world record claims. The job was made a little simpler with the deletion, since January 1977, of all imperial distances (bar the mile) from the world record lists. However, the introduction of new technology, such as fully automatic electrical timing, has added further complication to the job of ratification.

A new dimension to the IAAF's roles of organization and control has been the development and promotion of its own international competitions. These include the World Cup and Golden Events for track and field, the World Cross-Country Championships, the Lugano Cup for walking and in 1985 the first Marathon World Cup will be staged. The most important innovation has, however, been the athletics World Championships, first staged in Helsinki in 1983.

The fourth IAAF President, Italian Dr Primo Nebiolo, elected in 1981, has taken over during a crucial period as regards the future of international athletics. New IAAF eligibility rules, which allow athletes to benefit financially from athletics without compromising their 'amateur' status, go some way towards avoiding the potentially damaging aspects of commercialism and professionalism which might otherwise pervade the sport. Also, the recent widening of regulations banning the use of certain chemical substances (e.g. anabolic steroids) which artificially enhance athletic performance, and the setting up of laboratories for the detection of these substances in athletes participating in major competitions, is a step towards eradicating a particularly unsavoury development in athletics.

THE MODERN OLYMPIC GAMES

Much influenced by the ideas of Englishman Dr William P. Brookes, who formed an Olympian Society in Much Wenlock, Shropshire, as early as 1850, the French Baron Pierre de Coubertin is aptly described as the 'Founder of the Modern Olympic Games'. Commissioned by the French govenment in 1889 to examine the role of sport in the civilized world, in 1892 de Coubertin gave a lecture at the Sorbonne in Paris, where he made public his view that there should be a modern revival of the ancient Olympic Games. Through the French-man's sheer determination and unceasing effort his dream became a reality in June 1894 when at an international conference at the Sorbonne, attended by representatives from 13 countries, it was finally agreed that an Olympic Games would be staged at the beginning of four-yearly periods (Olympiads), commencing in 1896. At this same meeting the International Olympic Committee was founded to organize and control the Games and to decide suitable venues for future Olympic celebrations.

Originally, de Coubertin wanted the first Games to be staged in Paris in 1900 but it was eventually decided, in view of the Greeks' stronger historical and traditional claims, that it would be more appropriate to hold the first modern Olympic celebration in Athens. Chosen as the most suitable site for the first Games, the ancient Pan Athenaic Stadium of Herodis was restored in time for the official opening by King George of Greece on 6 April 1896—1503 years after the last of the ancient Olympic Games.

An estimated 80,000 spectators watched the Games, which included nine different sports. The athletics programme consisted of 12 events contested by 59 athletes from 10 nations. Overall, the standard of athletics was poor, mainly because of the inadequately surfaced track with its extremely tight bends and long straights. By far the strongest team was the 13-man American squad which won nine events in all, including the Greek speciality of the discus. The very first Olympic champion was American James Connolly who won

Part of the opening ceremony of the 1948 Olympic Games, held at Wembley, London.

THE IMPORTANT THING IN THE OLYMPIC GAMES IS NOT WINNING BUT TAKING PART. THE ESSENTIAL THING IN LIFE IS NOT CONQUERING BUT FIGHTING WELL

BARON de COUBERTIN

the triple jump on the first day with a modest leap, by today's standards, of 13.77 m (44 ft 11¾ in).

The highlight of the Games came on the fifth day when the final athletics event, the marathon, got under way. (The marathon race was originally devised to commemorate the legendary feat of the Greek soldier Pheidippides, who in 490 BC is said to have run from the plains of Marathon to the city of Athens—some 40 km (25 miles)—with news of the Greek army's victory over the Persians.) The Greeks had not achieved a single victory in the athletics events up to that point but thanks to a monumental effort by Spyridon Louis, a post office messenger, national pride was restored. Finishing over seven minutes ahead of his nearest rival in a field of 25 starters (21 of whom were Greeks), Louis completed the 40 km course, from the bridge of Marathon to the Olympic stadium, in 2 h. 58 min. 50 sec. to achieve one of the most famous victories in modern Olympic history.

Since those first Games the Olympics have become the most prestigious amateur sporting festival in the world, with a record number of 104 countries sending athletics teams to the 1972 Munich Olympic Games. The site for the celebration of the 1984 Games—the XXIIIrd Olympiad—is Los Angeles, in the USA.

21

OTHER MAJOR CONTESTS

International matches: An international athletics match is an event held over one to three days, in which teams representing two or more nations compete against each other in a number of standard track and field events. Points are awarded according to each athlete's finishing position in a particular event and each team's total points score, at the conclusion of the competition, decides their final positions in the match.

The earliest recorded instance of an international match goes back to 1876, when an England team competed against Ireland in Dublin, but it was not until 1921 that the first full-scale match occurred between a British team (styled 'England') and France in Paris. In between these years there was also an historic match, staged in New York, involving two virtually full international English and American teams, representing New York Athletic Club and London Athletics Club, in which the Americans won all eleven events. Surprisingly, the strongest athletics nation for most of this century, the USA, did not compete in their first full-scale dual international meeting (two-nation match) until they defeated Germany, then Europe's strongest athletics nation, in Berlin in 1938. Currently the most prestigious dual international match, held virtually every year, is that between the two athletics superpowers, the USA and USSR, who first crossed swords in Moscow in 1958.

The most important multi-national match competition in Europe is the biennial European Cup which was first staged in 1965. Since the early 1970s the East Germans have invariably dominated this competition. The IAAF World Cup is the biggest international match event worldwide. This three-day competition, for men and women, was first held in Düsseldorf in 1977 and differs from other international matches in that both national and continental teams take part.

European Championships: The driving force behind the introduction of athletics' European Championships was Hungarian IAAF Council member Szilard Stankovits, and the decision to stage the first Championships in Turin in 1934 was taken by the European Committee of the IAAF at a meeting in November 1932. Open to athletes eligible to represent any European nation, the inaugural European Championships attracted competitors from 16 countries, excluding Britain and the USSR. Women first took part in the Championships in 1938, though competing separately from the men in Vienna. Like the Olympics these Championships are traditionally staged once in four years, although the sequence was temporarily broken in 1969 and 1971.

Many athletes of European birth have figured among the greatest in the world and, consequently, the standard of athletic performance at the European Championships has been second only to that of the Olympic Games. At the most recent Championships, in Athens in 1982, no less than four world records were broken.

Other major European international athletics meetings include the annual European Indoor Championships, first sanctioned by the IAAF in 1970, and the European Junior Championships, which were officially recognized by the European Athletics Association in 1970.

British Empire and Commonwealth Games: The first major British Empire sporting festival was an 'Inter-Empire Championships', held at London's Crystal Palace in June 1911, but another 19 years were to elapse before the inaugural four-yearly British Empire Games were launched at Hamilton, Canada, in 1930. These Games were organized by M. M. Robinson, the manager of the 1928 Canadian Olympic team.

The British Empire Games Federation was founded in 1932 to organize and control the Games and at the London celebration of 1934 the Federation introduced the first women's athletics events. In fact, it was a woman, Australian Marjorie Jackson, who set the first athletics world records at the Games, in the 100 and 220 yards events at Auckland, New Zealand, in 1950. Since then many track and field world records have been set during the Games and numerous Commonwealth athletes have gone on to win Olympic medals.

British athletes have always competed as separate England, Wales, Scotland and Northern Ireland teams, partly to prevent almost total domination of the Games by a single British or United Kingdom team, but even so, England has collected more athletics medals than any other Commonwealth nation.

Pan-American Games: Although open only to athletes from the nations of the Americas, the Pan-American Games, which are the most important amateur sporting celebration throughout both continents of America, are closely modelled on the Olympics. Having been preceded by the Pan-American Exposition Games, staged at Dallas in 1937, the present Games were scheduled to start in 1942, only to be postponed due to World War II. The Pan-American Games finally got under way in 1951, the inaugural celebration taking place at Buenos Aires, Argentina, in February of that year.

The IAAF World Championships: Surprisingly, the most significant addition to the major international calendar has also been the most recent. Staged in Helsinki in August 1983, the inaugural IAAF World Championships attracted 1,570 of the world's finest male and female athletes from over 150 countries. The standard of athletic performance surpassed even that seen at the Olympics, and the continued success of this four-yearly venture, awarded to the city of Rome in 1987, must already be assured.

Other important games and championships: International athletics events in the form of major championships and as part of major games programmes are held on every continent on earth. The most significant of these are the African Games (inaugurated 1965) and Championships (since 1979), the Asian Games (1951), the Mediterranean Games (1951), and the Balkan Games (1948). Of greater international importance than all of these, however, are the World Student Games, first staged in Warsaw in 1924. Run by the Fédération Internationale du Sport Universitaire and open to athletes in full-time further education, these Games have seen the participation of many an Olympic gold medallist and spectators have witnessed numerous world-class athletics performances, including several world records.

DEVELOPMENT OF WOMEN'S ATHLETICS

The earliest recorded history of women's athletics goes back to the times of ancient Greece but the birth of female participation in modern athletics occurred in 1895, when women first competed in various athletics events at Vassar College in New York State, USA.

Undoubtedly the greatest pioneer for women's athletics was a Frenchwoman, Alice Milliat, who in 1917 formed the first official athletics governing body for women, the Fédération Feminine Sportive de France. Milliat was also instrumental in organizing the first women's international athletics celebration, the Monto Carlo Games, in 1921. Athletes from five nations, including Britain and France, took part and British girls won six of the 10 athletics events, the outstanding competitor being Briton Mary Lines who won the 60 and 250 metres sprints plus the long jump. These Games were held on only two subsequent occasions, in 1922 and 1923. Later in 1921 the first women's international match, between Belgium and France, took place in Brussels, although it was two years later before the first official match, between Britain and France, was held in Paris.

Alice Milliat's most significant claim to fame was the founding in October 1921 of the first international governing body for women's athletics, the Fédération Sportive Féminine Internationale. This organization's first notable achievement was to stage the 'Women's World Games' in Paris in 1922, as retaliation for the International Olympic Committee's refusal to include women's athletics events at the 1924 Paris Olympic Games. Held on a four-yearly basis this new international event proved to be a successful venture, continuing until 1934 when the London celebration attracted competitors from 19 nations. In the meantime the IOC finally relented, at their 1926 Congress, agreeing to include five women's athletics events (100 metres, 800 metres, 4×100 metres relay, high jump and discus) at the 1928 Amsterdam Olympic Games. Subsequent progress in this area can best be judged by the fact that there are 17 women's events on the athletics programme for the 1984 Los Angeles Olympics. Another of the FSFI's progressive innovations was to produce the first official list of women's world records (in 1927), which has since expanded to include 17 track and six field events records.

In the 1930s women's international athletics began to develop rapidly in several directions. The first women's international cross-country race was staged in Douai, France, in 1931, whilst in 1934 nine women's events were included in the British Empire Games athletics programme. The European Championships saw female participation for the first time in 1938, although the nine women's athletics events were held not in Paris alongside the men but at a separate venue in Vienna. It was not until the 1946 Championships in Oslo that men and women competed in the same arena.

In 1936, having completed the necessary groundwork to secure the future of women's international athletics, the FSFI finally merged with the IAAF, who now have total international control over the women's branch of the sport. One drawback to the development of women's athletics in more modern times has been the suspicion that certain distinguished female competitors were not, in truth, female. However, the introduction of chromosome count 'sex tests' in the mid-1960s has since resolved this problem.

From the modest beginnings women's athletics standards have progressed at an incredible rate, to a point where the top international female athletes are already achieving performances which would have been considered of international standard for the male athletes of no more than 40 or 50 years ago. Although it is unlikely that women will ever be able to compete on equal terms with men, primarily because of their physiological make-up, nevertheless the performance gap is still closing.

If anything, levels of performance in all branches of athletics are today progressing at a faster rate than ever before. In 1983, for example, of the standard major championship track and field events for which the official world records are recognized new record performances were achieved in 11 of the 21 men's events and 10 of the 16 women's events.

GROWTH OF INDOOR ATHLETICS

Surprisingly, the modern history of indoor athletics dates back well over 100 years and, as with the outdoor sport, the earliest pioneers in this particular branch of athletics were Great Britain and the United States. The very earliest indoor meeting was held at Ashburnham Hall, London, in November 1863, the athletics programme consisting of four running events from 100 to 880 yards and the triple jump. Just over five years later the New York Athletic Club held their first indoor meeting, on the site of the Empire City Skating Rink. The Americans were the first to stage an official national indoor championships, launching the inaugural US event in 1906 at the famous Madison Square Garden indoor arena (some 18 years after an unofficial championships meeting). The first US indoor championships for women occurred in 1927.

By the early 1920s there was already considerable public interest in indoor athletics in the USA, but following a barnstorming indoor tour by the great Finnish long distance runner Paavo Nurmi in 1925, it became a major spectator sport with indoor meetings attracting bigger crowds than many outdoor events. This new-found popularity encouraged many more athletes to take part in indoor meetings and, as a result, competition on the indoor circuit became as intense as that in the outdoor sport. Indoor athletics performances subsequently improved to a point where in certain events they rivalled equivalent outdoor standards. For instance, an indoor mile by American Glen Cunningham in 1938 timed at 4 min. 04.4 sec., was two seconds faster than the existing outdoor world record. The USA currently has many more indoor tracks than any other country, which include two of the biggest indoor facilities in the world. The huge Houston Astrodome houses a track of 322 m (352 yards) circuit, whilst the fieldhouse of Washington State University is big enough to stage indoor discus, hammer and even javelin competitions!

England followed the American example in 1935, becoming the first European country to hold national indoor championships, for both men and women. Wembley Pool was the venue for those early meetings which made use of a tiny flat $142\frac{1}{2}$ yard ($12\frac{1}{2}$ laps to the mile) track. A banked board track was installed in 1937 but the championships were discontinued, not to reappear again until 1962, in which year Britain played host to the world's first full international indoor match, between British and West German teams at the Wembley arena. In 1965 an aircraft hangar at RAF Cosford became the permanent home for British indoor athletics.

Indoor athletics began to take off in the rest of Europe during the 1950s and the inaugural European Indoor Games were held at Dortmund in March 1966. This event became the European Indoor Championships in 1970, in which year they were sanctioned by the IAAF, and since then the annual meetings have attracted many of Europe's finest athletes.

As yet there are no world championships for indoor athletics but it can only be a matter of time before such an event comes into being.

A 3000 metres race on an indoor track—Sebastian Coe at No. 6.

PROFESSIONAL ATHLETICS

Historical evidence suggests that paid athletes competed at the Olympic Games in ancient Greece, but it was not until the seventeenth century AD that professionalism first appeared in competitive athletics of the more modern era. In those days wagering on the outcome of foot races between the footmen servants of the gentry was a most popular pastime. During the nineteenth century professional athletics was more widespread than the developing amateur sport, with a number of organized meetings for professional athletes being staged in England and Scotland. Sprint handicap events were often held at Sheffield until the late nineteenth century and in 1870 one of the most famous professional athletics meetings, the Powderhall New Year Handicaps, was first staged in Edinburgh. The main attraction of the Powderhall event is a 120 yards (110 m) handicap sprint which has been worth up to £1,000 to the winner. A similar annual event, known as the Stawell Gift, began in Australia in 1877. This 130 yards (119 m) sprint handicap has even attracted former Olympic sprint champions in recent years.

Because of the money involved, competition in nineteenth-century professional athletics was intense and consequently the performances among the professional athletes were far superior to those of their amateur counterparts. For example, the English runner Walter George ran a mile in 4 min. 12¾ sec. as a professional in 1886; a performance that remained unsurpassed by an amateur until 1915.

In 1973 a newly-formed American organization, the International Track Association, attempted to introduce a major professional athletics circuit, enticing a number of leading international athletes away from the amateur ranks. The ITA successfully staged a number of indoor and outdoor meetings both in the USA and abroad but, eventually, falling attendances and a failure to attract new athletics stars resulted in the ITA's collapse in 1976.

Since the beginning of the 1980s several professional road races have been staged in the USA, although recent changes in the IAAF's eligibility rules have made it possible for amateur athletes to compete in such races, provided that they pay their winnings into strictly controlled trust funds.

ORGANIZATION OF ATHLETICS

It is probably true to say that the organization and administrative structure of the sport of athletics in the United Kingdom is more complex and fragmented than in any other major sport. The fundamental reasons for this go back to the very earliest beginnings of British athletics when several embryonic regional organizations battled for the overall control of the sport. The problem of national control seemed to have been solved, for England and Wales at least, with the formation, in 1880, of the Amateur Athletic Association (AAA—called the 3A's) but even today that body's constituent area associations, jealous of their regional autonomy, remain pretty much a law unto themselves. The development of women's athletics and the international sport created further problems which resulted in the athletics governing bodies of Scotland and Northern Ireland and England's women athletes going their own way.

Eventually, in 1932, representatives from the various governing bodies were persuaded to come together to form what later became the British Amateur Athletic Board (BAAB). As a confederation of all the athletics associations of Great Britain and Northern Ireland, the BAAB took over from the AAA as the single body eligible to represent the UK as an affiliated member of the IAAF, but the Board's powers extended only to matters concerning international athletics: control of the domestic sport remained firmly in the hands of the associations which it represented.

Today the constituent members of the BAAB include the AAA, the Women's Amateur Athletic Association (WAAA), the separate men's and women's AAAs of Scotland, Wales

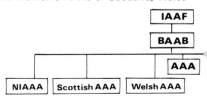

and Northern Ireland and two international athlete's representatives, although only the Associations can vote on important issues raised at the BAAB's annual general meeting.

The BAAB's most important responsibilities include control of international athletics in the UK and selection and management of international teams representing Britain in major international competitions, such as the Olympic Games, and in matches against other IAAF member nations. In addition, the BAAB administers the UK Coaching Scheme, a responsibility which it took over from the AAA in 1970, and since 1977 has promoted athletics' UK National Championships.

Another of the BAAB's responsibilities is ratification of UK National and All-Comers athletics records. Only performances set by athletes eligible to represent the United Kingdom in international competition qualify for the former category of records, whereas athletes from any nation can qualify for the latter category, provided their performances are set in the UK.

The BAAB's substantial administrative and coaching expenses are funded through generous sponsorship of its international match programme as well as through television fees, Sports Council grants, meeting gate receipts and now, a percentage from the top athletes' trust funds.

Theoretically, the AAA's responsibilities nowadays extend only to the running of men's athletics at national level in England and Wales. In fact, the AAA also organizes its own international match programme, as do the Scottish, Welsh and Northern Ireland Associations, although only the BAAB strictly qualifies to take on such duties as Britain's sole affiliated member of the IAAF. Apparently the Federation tolerates this blatant disregard for its international rules and regulations on 'historical' grounds. Also, the AAA runs its

This chart of the various governing bodies involved in the running of athletics in the United Kingdom illustrates the complexity of the organizational structure of the sport.

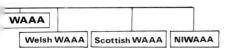

own annual track and field championships, the AAA Championships, which have always been regarded as the major domestic athletics championships in the UK and still carry the greatest prestige, despite the existence of the BAAB's championships.

Unlike the BAAB, the AAA has its own affiliated member athletics clubs, numbering well over a thousand, and its own competition rules, though these do not differ materially from the IAAF rules and regulations.

A separate category of athletics records under the title of AAA National records are listed and ratified by the AAA. This category covers performances achieved in England and Wales by athletes born in those countries or who are *bona fide* members of athletics clubs under the jurisdiction of the AAA and whose fathers were born in England or Wales.

The AAA receives its funds from much the same sources as the BAAB but in addition receives fees from all of its member clubs and currently the AAA enjoys a far healthier financial position than the theoretically more influential BAAB.

The seven other main associations in the UK are responsible for the general organization of athletics within their areas and each promotes its own national athletics championships.

As if this set-up were not complicated enough the AAA and WAAA are further subdivided into Northern, Midlands and Southern Associations, which control their own areas and run annual Area championships. The English Cross-Country Union is another subdivision of the AAA, responsible for administering its own branch of athletics and is itself subdivided into area associations. All the other main associ-

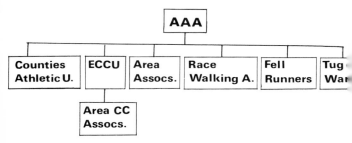

ations also have their own cross-country governing bodies. Other semi-autonomous subdivisions of the AAA include the Counties Athletic Union, which holds its own annual Inter-Counties Championships, and the Race Walking Association.

Despite the fact that the early development of modern athletics in the United States goes back almost as far as does the British history of the sport, the organization of American athletics is relatively uncomplicated compared to the British system. Since 1888, the year in which the Amateur Athletic Union of America (known as the AAU) was founded, American athletics has been administered by a single major governing body. All amateur sport in the USA is under the control of the AAU but in 1979 the responsibility for athletics was relinquished in favour of a newly formed body, The Athletics Congress of the USA (known as TAC).

The only branch of American athletics that TAC does not totally control is College athletics. However, the American University and College athletics programme provides such superior facilities for coaching, training and competition that the vast majority of the country's top athletes are a product of the Collegiate athletics set-up and are, therefore, under the jurisdiction of the National Collegiate Athletic Association. The standard of athletics at the NCAA's annual track and field championships rivals even that of TAC's National Championships and many college athletes represent their country in major international events such as the Olympics, although it is TAC that controls their participation in international competition.

In all other IAAF member nations the athletics organization is even simpler that the US system, with only the governing body affiliated to the IAAF maintaining total control of the sport in their own countries.

The most influential of the major men's and women's UK associations, the AAA and WAAA, are further subdivided into several semi-autonomous governing bodies.

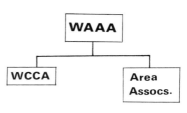

THE ATHLETICS STADIUM

Before construction is even begun on a new athletics stadium, certain factors have to be taken into consideration. For example, the track must be laid on a perfectly level site, for even a virtually unnoticeable slope might invalidate any track or field event record performances achieved in the new arena. Other factors, such as prevailing wind directions and the position of the afternoon sun, are also important. Unhelpful wind conditions can adversely affect a number of athletics events, whilst competitors having constantly to face into the sun during their events are obviously at a disadvantage.

The track layout

The typical outdoor athletics running track is almost elliptical in shape, with two parallel straights of around 80 m (262 ft) in length and two semicircular bends, all of which are bordered by a kerb on the track's inside edge. Since athletics track events are almost universally run over metric distances—indoor track events on the USA are the major exception—the standard track is a circuit of 400 m (438 yd). The track is divided into lanes (usually 8 but sometimes 9 lanes are used for major competition) to separate individual runners in hurdles and sprint races. These lanes are numbered consecutively from the inside outwards and each measures a minimum of 1.22 m (4 ft) in width.

In all races the athletes run in a counter-clockwise direction with the track's inside kerb always to the left and all track events, regardless of length, share the same finish line at the end of the homestraight (in front of the main stand). The 100 metres sprint and 100 and 110 metres hurdles events are run entirely on the homestraight, whilst those races longer than the 110 metres start at various points around the track (see diagram opposite).

Races which are run in lanes and incorporate at least one bend involve certain complications. On a standard track the arrangement of the lanes, one outside another, results in each lane being several metres longer, due to the wider bends, than the one inside it. These differences in length must be adjusted by way of a staggered start, so that each athlete runs an identical race distance. In the 400 metres event only the

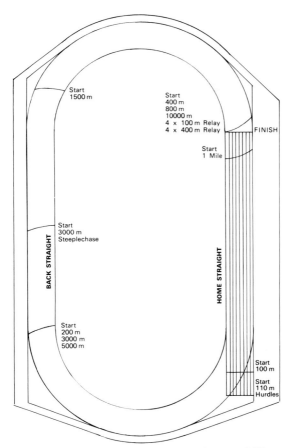

Although, as shown, the start lines for track races of different lengths are situated at various points around the standard 400 metres track, all races share the same finish.

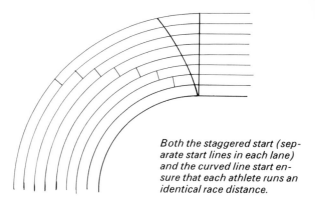

Both the staggered start (separate start lines in each lane) and the curved line start ensure that each athlete runs an identical race distance.

runner on the inside lane starts and finishes at the same point on the track, for only that lane measures exactly 400 m. The scratch line, or start line, in lane 2 is situated some 7 m (23 ft) or so (depending on the overall dimensions of the track) beyond the scratch line in lane 1 and, similarly, the scratch lines in the outer lanes are an equal distance beyond those of the lanes inside them (see diagram above). This staggered start arrangement gives the impression that athletes starting on the outside lanes have a distance advantage over those on the inside, yet each scratch line is an equal distance from the finish line.

Staggered starts are not required in distance events where the entire race is run only on the inside lane, although the runners do start from a curved scratch line drawn across the track (see diagram above), so that athletes starting furthest from the inside lane run no more than the exact race distance. Details of the track markings and staggers for the sprint relays are given on pages 98 to 101.

The infield layout
The majority of the field event installations are located within the confines of the grass-covered stadium infield, where their placement conforms to a standard plan (see diagram opposite), though there are minor variations.

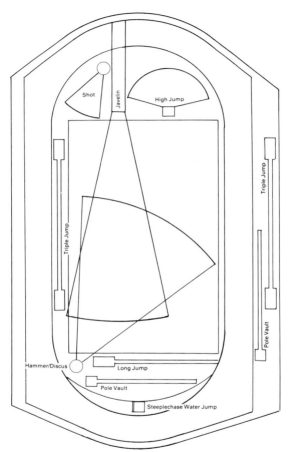

The exact positioning of the field event facilities within the arena may vary from one stadium to another but the basic dimensions and specifications are always the same.

The basic installations for the jumping events, some of which may be located just outside the main track, consist of a runway and a landing area. In the case of the long and triple jumps and the pole vault the runways, which are constructed of the same material as the track (see page 39), measure a minimum of 40 m in length by 1.22 m wide (131×4 ft). The landing area for the horizontal jumps is a permanently sited sand-filled pit, located at the end of the runway, measuring 2.75 m wide by 9 or 10 m in length (9×33 ft). For the vertical jumping events (high jump and pole vault) the landing area consists of a foam rubber mattress up to 1 m (3 ft) thick, measuring 5.0 m (16 ft) square for the pole vault and 5×3 m (16×10 ft) for the high jump, on to which the athlete lands when jumping. The high jump facilities are always located on the infield and the runway is in the shape of a wide, flat, almost semicircular fan with a minimum radius of 15 m (49 ft).

The installations and facilities for the throwing events take up by far the greater part of the infield, requiring a throwing area and a designated area within which the throwing implement must land. In the shot put, discus and hammer throwing events the implement is launched from a flat concrete circle, which measures 2.5 m (8 ft $2\frac{1}{2}$ in) in diameter for the discus but is smaller, at 2.135 m (7 ft) diameter, for the other two events. The immediate throwing areas for the potentially dangerous discus and hammer events are partially surrounded by permanently sited 4 m (12 ft) high cages. Landing areas for throwing implements are bounded by straight white lines which radiate from the throwing circles to form 40° landing sectors. The shot put sector takes up least space, for even international putters rarely send the shot more than 22 m (72 ft) beyond the circle. The discus and hammer, on the other hand, may travel 70 and 80 m (230 and 262 ft), respectively, and although these events may share the same throwing area and sector, they still occupy the entire centre of the infield when in progress.

Unlike the other throws the javelin event utilizes a runway measuring around 36.5 m in length and 4 m in width (120×13 ft), whilst the throwing sector is narrower at around 29°. However, with the top male throwers regularly producing 90 m (295 ft) throws the javelin facilities extend virtually the full length of the infield.

STADIUM: *TRACK SURFACES*

One of the most significant technological advances in the sport of athletics in recent years has been the development of the artificial 'all-weather', surface track. The idea for artificial track surfaces goes back more than 30 years when rubberized asphalt surfaces were first developed by the US Rubber Reclaiming Co., who laid such a track at Buffalo, New York State, in 1950. The popular 'Tartan' artificial track surfaces were developed from 1963 by American William McKnight and they were first used for major international athletics events at the 1967 Pan-American and 1968 Olympic Games.

A variety of different track surfaces were in use prior to the arrival of artificial surfaces, the most common being cinder tracks. These were preferred for major athletics events since they served as excellent running surfaces when well maintained. However they had the drawback that in wet weather they became flooded and soft, adversely affecting all track performances. Grass tracks have been used even for major athletics competitions in countries with hot climates such as Australia and New Zealand but, again, wet weather can render this type of surface virtually unusable. Many cinder and clay tracks are still in use, particularly in underdeveloped countries, due to the high cost of installing artificial surfaces.

Today there are numerous companies marketing many different types of artificial surfaces, although all are composed of similar complex polymer compounds. The most costly surfaces are those consisting either of prefabricated plastic sheets bonded with adhesives to a sub-base, or a sub-base onto which has been spread a synthetic rubber solution that solidifies to form a resilient rubberized surface. These normally dark track surfaces are sprayed with textured paint to give them their attractive colours. Britain's first 'Tartan' track was that laid at Crystal Palace, London. This track consists of a tarmac sub-base covered with a porous layer of rubber particles mixed with a binding agent.

The main advantage of 'all-weather' tracks is that they are, of course, completely weather resistant and extremely hardwearing. Equally important, though, they provide a firm yet springy running surface which enhances athletic performance.

STADIUM: *WIND GAUGE*

During sprinting and hurdles events up to and including 200 metres and the horizontal jumps, strong winds can have a material effect on an athlete's performance. A strong following wind can push the sprinter to faster times and propel the jumper greater distances. Athletics performances achieved with the aid of following winds over a certain speed are, therefore, deemed to be wind-assisted and, as such, cannot be accepted for record purposes. For the above-mentioned events following wind speeds in excess of 2 metres per second would invalidate record performances. Where these events occur in multi-events competitions the limit is higher at 4 m/sec.

To determine whether a performance was aided by excessive wind-assistance wind speeds are measured with a funnel-shaped wind gauge apparatus. The wind gauge, which rests on a tripod, can be seen alongside the inside lane of the track, halfway down the homestraight, or alongside the horizontal jumps runway 20 m (66 ft) from the take-off board, so that the funnel is parallel to the running or jumping direction. Then, while the sprinters are running the length of the straight, or the jumper is running up and jumping, the wind velocity blowing through the funnel in either direction during that time is automatically measured. The most up-to-date gauges can be set to operate for a fixed period of time (i.e. 5 sec. for the jumps, 10 sec. for the sprints) and the readout is given as the average wind speed in metres per second.

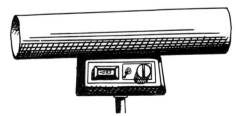

Wind gauge apparatus: the velocity of the wind passing through the funnel is electronically measured and the result shown on the digital display.

STADIUM: *STARTER'S GUN*

First used in athletics in 1876, the starter's gun, or pistol, still proves to be the most effective method of starting any running event, from a short sprint event to a long distance road race. Starter's pistols of .22 or .32 calibre are commonly used, firing blank cartridges that give a particularly loud, sharp report, which is especially important when starting a large field such as for a marathon.

At the start of a sprint race on the track it is crucial that all competitors should hear the gun simultaneously. Since the starter fires his pistol from a position further away from the athletes in the outside lanes than those on the inside, the sound inevitably takes a fraction longer to reach the furthest athletes (unless some form of loudspeaker system specifically for the start is in use), who would be at an even greater disadvantage if the starting signal were not clearly audible.

The starter's gun can also be used to recall athletes immediately after the start of a race where a competitor has committed a false start, thus the spectators will invariably see the starter carry a pistol in each hand. At major athletics events where automatic timing is in operation, the firing of the starter's gun also serves to trigger the timing mechanism to which it is electronically linked (see p. 42).

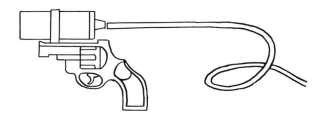

The starter's gun may be electronically connected to an automatic timing system so that when the gun is fired the timing mechanism is instantaneously triggered.

STADIUM: *PHOTO-FINISH EQUIPMENT*

Ever since the early days of modern athletics a major problem for officials has been the correct placing of competitors at the finish of a close race, particularly in the short sprints. Nowadays, with top male sprinters operating at speeds close to 44 km/h (27 mph), it is impossible for the naked eye to be able to determine accurately the finishing sequence of runners in a blanket finish. This problem was finally solved with the development of the modern photo-finish camera, which came into general use in the 1940s and is now an essential piece of equipment at all major athletics events. Photo-finish cameras of one type or another have been in use since the turn of the century but these were far less reliable than the highly sophisticated and accurate cameras available today.

Unlike an ordinary camera the photo-finish camera does not have a shutter and does not take a single picture of the finish of a race. Instead, it has a very narrow slit lens which photographs an area of the finish no more than 5–10 cm (2–4 in) across. The camera uses a continuous strip of film that moves across the lens at a speed proportionate to the speed of the object being photographed, and in this way the camera records the arrival of each competitor at the finish line. Therefore, the space between the athletes on a photo-finish photograph represents the time elapsed between the arrival of each of them at the line, rather than the actual distance between them. The advantage of the photo-finish photograph over an ordinary photo is that it shows a runner's relative finishing position in a race the split second that he crosses the line. An ordinary picture, taken as the first finisher crosses the line, only gives the relative positions of other runners whilst they are still some distance from the finish. The photo-finish equipment is capable of producing developed negatives in under a minute.

The photo-finish equipment also doubles up as an electronic timing device, recording competitors' finishing times to one-hundredth of a second. The photo-finish timing mechanism is triggered by the firing of the starter's gun and in the most sophisticated systems an electronic device inscribes the times,

In this photo-finish of a sprint race it is possible both to accurately determine each athlete's finishing position and to ascertain individual finishing times within 1/100th of a second.

down to 0.01 sec., on to the film itself. This gives a developed photograph which shows both the relative race positions of the finishing athletes and a time scale, at the top or bottom of the photo, that gives the exact times when each runner's torso crossed the finish line.

It is generally accepted that fully automatic electronic timing is more accurate than manual timing. This is because the human timekeeper has a tendency to anticipate the athletes' finish, which results in faster times than on automatic timing. The average accepted time differences between manual and automatic timing is 0.24 sec. for the 200 metres and shorter sprints and 0.14 sec. for races over the 200 metres. In view of this discrepancy, the IAAF has ruled that as from 1977 only sprint performances recorded by fully automatic timing can be recognized for world record purposes.

STADIUM: *ELECTRONIC SCOREBOARD*

400 M HURDLES		00:47.82	WR
FINAL		00:47.82	OR
OMEGA			
1 MOSES	USA	00:47.64	WR
2 SHINE	USA	00:48.69	
3 GAVRILYENKO	URS	00:49.45	
4 WHEELER	USA	00:49.86	
5 CARVALHO	POR	00:49.94	
6 BRATANOV	BUL	00:50.03	
7 DAMASO	CUB	00:50.19	
8 PASCOE	GBR	00:51.29	

The information display facilities at many of the most modern athletics arenas are more sophisticated and up to date than at the major venues for most other sports. One, or possibly two, immense electronic scoreboards, operated from a control centre, normally serve as the main information display units at major athletics events. Although these scoreboards often differ in design they all exhibit similar basic features, specifically a clock and a display face that is made up of perhaps several thousand light bulbs, sections of which can be independently illuminated to form letters and numbers on the board.

The kind of information usually displayed on the scoreboard includes heat and lane draws in each track event; competitors' jumping or throwing order in field events; and competition results for individual athletes and their final placings in each event. The most modern information systems utilize a computer, enabling results to be displayed within minutes, or even seconds, of the conclusion of an event. Many scoreboards also have a built-in timing mechanism, so that elapsed and final times can be displayed during and immediately after track events. The latest scoreboards incorporate a TV screen facility that can show live pictures of events in progress, and even slow-motion replays following the action.

STADIUM: *FIELD EVENT SCOREBOARDS AND CLOCKS*

In addition to the main scoreboard, athletics stadium information display facilities also include field event scoreboards. These relatively small moveable units are generally located behind the throwing areas for throwing events and close to the runways for jumping events.

The manually-operated flap information display type of event scoreboards have been virtually replaced by electronic units, but with both types the information displayed includes the competition number of the athlete throwing or jumping; the distance or height achieved after a valid trial or attempt (the board also indicates a foul jump/throw); and the number of jumps per round or throws already taken by the athlete in the competition. The use of field event scoreboards enables the spectator to follow the progress of an entire field event competition from start to finish. At best, the main scoreboard will only display details of field events at the end of each round of attempts or, more likely, at the conclusion of the competition.

The field events clocks are placed in suitable positions on the infield, where they can be used to time individual athletes' attempts during a competition. There are specific regulations governing how long a competitor may take to execute a jump or throw, so that particularly the more involved events can be completed in reasonable time. An athlete who does not take his attempt within the time limit may be deemed to have committed a foul trial. These time limits are 2 minutes for an attempt in the pole vault and $1\frac{1}{2}$ minutes for all other field events.

Opposite above: *Main scoreboard displaying race results.*
Right: *Field event scoreboard showing competition round, the athlete's competition number and the performance achieved in metres.*

STADIUM: *FIELD EVENT MEASURING DEVICES*

The measurement of jumps and throws in field events is one area of athletics in which modern technology plays a big part. Where modern measuring equipment is not available, the simple steel tape is still the most reliable tool for accurate measurement, but the latest optical measuring devices are quicker and easier to use.

The optical measuring equipment used for the horizontal jumps consists of a telescopic gun sight pivoted on a carriage (see illustration below) which slides along a beam running parallel to the landing pit. To take a measurement, a marker is placed in the sand at the point where the jumper has landed and the telescopic sight is lined up with the marker. The instrument then takes its reading from a datum point, determined when the equipment is installed, and displays the measurement on a digital readout. The unit can be automatically switched to long or triple jump measurement.

Modern measuring apparatus for the throwing events is extremely sophisticated and accurate, utilizing an infra-red laser system to take measurements, from the throwing implement's point of impact to the measuring apparatus and from the apparatus to a fixed datum point at the throwing area scratch line, which are then used, by a computer, to calculate the exact throwing distance.

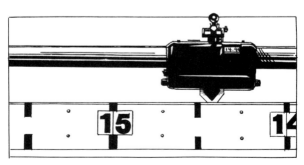

STADIUM: *STARTING BLOCKS*

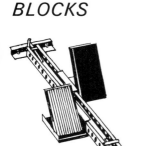

Used in conjunction with starting blocks (left), *a false start detector illuminates lights on an indicator box* (right) *when triggered.*

Starting blocks are a piece of equipment used by sprinters and hurdlers in races up to and including the 400 metres, and on the first leg of all sprint relays to help the athlete get a good, fast start. Perfected in 1927 by Americans George Bresnahan and William Tuttle, starting blocks are of the same basic design today as the original models. The standard type of starting blocks consist of a metal frame (centre bar) and a pair of angled adjustable foot plates, one on either side of the frame. One of these foot plates is generally positioned further forward and at a shallower angle than the other, so that the sprinter can press his feet flat against them when assuming the typical crouched starting position. The starting blocks are screwed firmly to the track, just behind the scratch line, so as to give the sprinter a solid base to push off from when the starter's gun fires. In the 400 metres event, where the athletes run a complete circuit of the track, the officials have to be quick to remove the starting blocks from the track during the race before the runners arrive back at the original starting positions.

At major athletics events such as the Olympics, the official starting blocks have a built-in electronic false start detector which indicates if a sprinter's foot has left the blocks before the gun has fired.

THE WELL-DRESSED ATHLETE

Despite the ever-changing dictates of fashion, the basic competition and training wear for male and female athletes, whether for running or field events, tends to remain very much the same. IAAF regulations do, however, stipulate that competition clothing should be made of a material that is non-transparent even when wet and should be clean and so designed and worn as not to be 'objectionable'.

Clothing

The standard vests and shorts are worn in competition by sprinters, distance runners, jumpers and throwers alike and for every event this clothing needs to be sufficiently loose and brief to allow complete freedom of leg and arm movement. In cold weather competitors might wear a tee shirt underneath the vest and, in the case of cross-country runners, even tights may be worn under shorts as added insulation against particularly bad weather during a race. In contrast, marathon runners competing in warm summer weather often wear mesh vests, which allow the air to reach and cool the skin more efficiently, whilst an all-white strip is generally favoured as it reflects the sunlight.

An indispensable item of clothing worn by athletes when warming up for competition or during training, especially in cold weather, is the tracksuit. Consisting of trousers and a top, the tracksuit completely covers the wearer's arms and legs, helping to retain body heat and thereby reducing the chances of muscle injuries that can occur when cold muscles are worked too hard too quickly. Some athletes may further insulate themselves against bad weather when training and warming up by wearing several layers of clothing, including tights and similar garments, underneath their tracksuit. Waterproof plastic rain suits are generally worn over tracksuits in wet and windy weather. A nylon or cotton tracksuit alone would soon become saturated in the rain making it virtually impossible for the wearer to get warm.

There is little need for variety in the style of athletics clothing for competition and training but the requirements of different events necessitate a wide range of specialized footwear.

Footwear

So diverse are the many activities which go to make up the sport of athletics, that an equally diverse range of footwear has been developed over the years to adapt to the special requirements of particular events. Regardless of the actual external design of the different types of footwear, the shoe sole must not be more than 13 mm ($\frac{1}{2}$ in) thick and for most events the heel of the shoe must not be more than 6 mm ($\frac{1}{4}$ in) thicker than the sole.

Spiked running shoes (spikes), which are designed to give added stability and grip on the running surface, are worn for all running events on the track and all jumping events. This type of shoe normally has screw-in metal spikes so that the number, position and length of spikes used can be varied to suit particular events and running surfaces. Short spikes (up to 12 mm) are most suitable for use on artificial surfaces to avoid damaging the track, but on loose cinder surfaces spikes of anything up to 25 mm (1 in) in length would be necessary. Spiked shoes for track events and the horizontal jumps have a maximum of six spikes, located only in the sole. Among track athletes the sprinters are most reliant on good foot stability when running, especially if negotiating bends at high speed, so they might use slightly longer spikes than would distance runners, and whereas the sprinter would always have the maximum allowable number of spikes in each shoe, the distance runner might use only four in each.

Specialized long jumping shoes have a ribbed sole to improve the jumper's grip on the smooth take-off board, whilst the triple jump shoe has a flat heel that better distributes the pressure on impact when jumping. In addition, horizontal jumpers can use padding or plastic heel cups inside the shoe to build the heel up to a maximum thickness of 25 mm for extra cushioning. In the case of the vertical jumps the spiked shoes used for pole vaulting are little different from those used for track events but high jump shoes are more specialized. Here, the shoe worn on the take-off foot has spikes in the heel (four maximum) as well as the sole. These additional spikes are necessary so that both the heel and sole of the take-off foot make firm contact with the ground at the point of take-off. Some high jumpers only have spikes in the shoe worn on the take-off foot, for the other foot must be able to swing through and upwards at the point of take-off without catching on the ground. For all track and jumping events the competitors would normally wear flat rubber-soled shoes to warm up in, changing into their spikes at the start of the event.

With the exception of the javelin, shoes for the throwing events do not have spikes. The soles of the shoes for the shot, discus and hammer events should be smooth and ideally of convex section so that the thrower (particularly in the discus and hammer) can turn easily in the throwing circle. The javelin thrower requires the most specialized footwear, in the form of high-sided boots which are essential to support the thrower's ankles. Javelin boots also have spikes in both the heel and sole to improve grip on the runway.

The greatest range in styles and design of athletics footwear is to be found in the road running branch of the sport. In general, road running shoes tend to be lightweight, yet hard wearing, with plenty of padding and cushioning, particularly around the heel, to improve shock absorption and reduce wear and tear on the runner's legs. The rubber soles of road shoes come in several designs but among the most popular, because of their better resilience and traction, are the waffle-sole variety, which appear as a lattice-work of small square studs. Cross-country shoes are similar to those used for road running except that the soles are composed of small round studs, rather like those on football boots. Race walkers also wear rubber-soled shoes but since the walker's heels tend to take a great deal of pounding, the heels on race walking shoes can be as much as 26 mm in thickness.

THE COMPETITION

Participating in a major athletics competition may represent the culmination of an athlete's efforts over perhaps years of training. Yet all that hard work can be undone in seconds if a competitor is not prepared both mentally and physically on the day of the event. Everything that the athlete has learned about the techniques and tactics of his particular event must be condensed into maybe just a moment of intense activity—combined with calm controlled efficiency—if he is to have any chance of progressing through to the final stages of competition and achieving ultimate victory. On top of everything else the athlete must adhere to the rules and regulations governing even relatively minor aspects of the competition, to avoid last-minute upsets which could destroy concentration and adversely affect his performance.

Warming up for competition

In order for muscles to work with optimum efficiency during physical activity they must be supple and warm. If an athlete does not stretch and work his muscles before subjecting them to severe stress through running, jumping and throwing, then he is likely to damage or even tear the muscle fibres. Tendons are also susceptible to injury, the hamstrings (tendons behind the knees) being particularly vulnerable in sprinters and hurdlers. Warming up for at least 30 minutes before competition is, therefore, vital.

For events run on the flat, warming up consists of steady jogging to warm the muscles, followed by faster running, or striding, to stretch and loosen them. Hurdlers, jumpers and throwers put much more emphasis on stretching and mobility exercises (callisthenics) to keep leg, hip, back, shoulder and arm muscles supple. Many track and field sports complexes have a training track or similar area close by the main arena where athletes can warm up before their events and, often, runners can be seen striding along the main track backstraight as they add the finishing touches to their preparations just before a race gets underway.

Identifying competitors and their teams

During a typical athletics meeting there may be any number

of athletes competing at one and the same time, from eight individuals in a track or field event final to several hundreds, or even thousands, during a cross-country or road race. Whatever the number, it is essential that the officials know who each individual is, particularly for recording results. For this reason each athlete is allotted a separate competition number which will appear alongside his name and club or team in the meeting programme, published for the information of the officials and spectators alike. IAAF regulations require that, with the exception of pole vaulters and high jumpers, all competitors must wear the numbers provided both on the front and back of their competition vests, making identification easier. In addition, where photo-finish equipment is in operation, competitors are also required to display their numbers on the sides of their shorts so that they are identifiable on the photo-finish photograph. Athletes not displaying numbers in the required manner can be prevented from taking part in an event.

The members of different teams, whether they be club teams in a league match or national teams in a major international championships, are identifiable by the team colours displayed on their vests and shorts. Where a points scoring system is employed to determine the winning team in a match it is imperative that officials should know to which team athletes in each event belong.

Event heats and qualifying competitions

In major track and field meetings the number of competitors entered for the majority of events is usually too large to be able to stage straight finals to decide the winners. It is therefore necessary to hold preliminary competitions in these events in order to eliminate a proportion of the entrants and thereby arrive at more manageable numbers for the finals. In the Olympic Games, for example, a number of heats are staged in all track events up to and including the 10,000 metres, and in each heat perhaps the first 2 or 3 finishers and the next 3 or 4 fastest athletes over all of the heats go through to the final or to the next round of heats. In this way the field is eventually reduced to between 8 to 12 finalists, depending on the event.

For the field events preliminary qualifying competitions

may precede the finals. In the high jump and pole vault the competitors would be required to clear a predetermined height in order to qualify for the final, whereas in the throwing events and the horizontal jumps they would have to achieve a certain predetermined throwing or jumping distance. Where too few competitors actually achieve the qualifying heights or distances, those falling just short of the qualifying limits would be added to the final pool. Performances set up in the qualifying competitions, including any records, have no bearing on the results of the event finals.

False starts, no jumps and no throws
Even after a competitor has reached an event final there is still the possibility that he might be eliminated from the competition before he has had the opportunity to show his full potential.

In all track events, but particularly in the sprints and hurdles races, the nervous athlete runs the risk of committing a false start by moving before the starter's gun has fired at the beginning of a race. A competitor receives only a caution for a first false start but if he commits a second, he is effectively eliminated without even starting the race. Similarly, field event athletes may face elimination from the competition if their technical skills are not at their sharpest. If a high jumper or pole vaulter fails to clear a height in three consecutive attempts he is eliminated, although he will still be credited with the last height actually cleared. Where the throws and horizontal jumps are concerned there is less likelihood of a competitor failing to register a valid jump or throw, particularly in a competition where each athlete has a maximum of six trials. In a major contest, however, where only the leading eight individuals after three trials are permitted three more trials, there is a greater risk of an athlete failing to register a mark and being eliminated.

Drugs and doping
A most worrying aspect of athletic competition today is the spreading use among athletes of drugs which artificially improve athletic performance. Since the 1950s substances such as amphetamines, which stimulate the nervous system and delay the onset of fatigue, are known to have been used

by individuals throughout the sports world. More recently chemical substances known as anabolic steroids, which enhance muscle growth and enable the user to train more intensely, have arrived on the sports scene and up until recently were virtually undetectable in the human body, since they so closely resemble naturally occurring male hormones. Nowadays, athletes using steroids are avoiding detection by switching to the naturally occurring male hormone testosterone several weeks before a major competition.

Apart from the fact that drugs give the user an unfair advantage in competition, they can also have harmful side-effects. The IAAF has banned the use of amphetamines, anabolic steroids and other substances and, in addition, various clinical testing procedures have been devised to detect doping substances in the body. Also, sophisticated doping control laboratories have been set up so that at all major international athletics meetings urine samples from medal winners and other randomly selected athletes can be tested for drugs. Since 1968 many athletes, including runners, jumpers and throwers, have been found to have taken illegal doping substances and, nowadays, offenders face at least a 12-month suspension from all major athletics competitions on the strength of a positive doping test.

Medal ceremonies

During a major international track and field athletics meeting the completion of each event final is normally followed by a medal presentation ceremony. Gold, silver and bronze medals are awarded to the athletes placing first, second and third, respectively, in each event during these ceremonies, which usually take place on the infield close to the homestraight. The awarding of these highly valued medals serves to commemorate the individual athlete's performances in major competition.

THE OFFICIALS

One of the problems associated with a sport as complex as athletics is that of the organization and efficient running of a competition, such as a track and field meeting, in which perhaps three or more separate events might be in progress at any one time. It is, of course, the athletes that the spectator comes to watch but both the athletes and the spectators have the many officials, present at every type of athletics contest, to thank for making it all possible. The officials, who can be seen posted around the stadium track and infield during a meeting, voluntarily give of their time and effort, without payment, to ensure that the athletics programme runs smoothly and on time for the convenience of the competitors and spectators alike. Given below are details of the scope of essential duties undertaken by the various officials normally present at a track and field meeting.

The technical manager (clerk of the course)

The technical manager is primarily responsible for ensuring that track markings, throwing circles, sectors and landing areas for the jumps are correctly laid out and that equipment such as steeplechase barriers and hurdles are available when required. He also ensures that throwing implements conform to official specifications and that items such as high jump and pole vault bars are available.

The technical manager may also be required to ensure that the track and infield are kept clear of everyone except authorized officials and competing athletes. In addition, he must endeavour to keep the programme of events running to schedule.

Referees

It is usual for two referees to be appointed, one to preside over the track events and the other the field events, although their duties are basically the same. In each case the referees ensure that all the relevant technical rules applying to their allotted events are observed. Other responsibilities include allocating specific duties to the judges and umpires and, in the case of the field events, ensuring that all competitors are aware of how many trials they may be permitted, or what heights they will be required to attempt in the high jump and pole vault.

The referee must deal with any disputed points or protests arising during competition, interpreting and applying the official rules to resolve such problems or, where there is no provision in the rules, using his discretion to arrive at an acceptable solution. For example, if at any stage there is a disagreement between the judges as to the finishing positions of competitors in a particular race, the referee acts as an adjudicator to settle the issue. Where necessary the referee also has the authority to caution or even disqualify any competitor guilty of improper conduct during an event.

Finally, the referee must check and verify all final results and, where a record is achieved in a field event, he should check measurements and implements used.

Judges

Judges are appointed by the meeting organizers to judge both the track and field events.

The track judges are responsible for deciding the order in which competitors finish in a race. To do this efficiently they must all operate from the same side of the track, taking up positions level with the finishing posts, no more than 5 m (16 ft) away from the inside track kerb. The judges are usually seated on a tiered stand so that each of them has a clear view of the finish. Each judge is responsible for placing one or more finishers in a race and where they cannot agree, the matter is referred to the track referee to decide.

The field judges are allocated various duties which include indicating whether a trial in any field event is a foul or a valid trial, by raising either a red or a white flag, respectively; measuring and recording each valid trial during a competition; and ensuring that the individual athletes compete in the correct order during every round of the competition.

In the high jump and pole vault the judges must measure the height of the bar every time it is raised and again after a successful jump where a record has been attempted.

Umpires

The umpires are track officials who are appointed to watch for and report to the track referee any infringements of the competition rules pertaining to particular track events. The umpires are posted around the track at the most appropriate positions for the race being observed. The most likely infringements include athletes running out of their allotted lanes or failing to clear obstacles correctly in the steeplechase and hurdles races, and relay teams failing to execute a changeover within the boundaries of the track changeover zones. An infringement is indicated by the raising of a red flag.

The starter
The starter, who has the sole charge and responsibility for the start of all track races, is easily recognizable by his red blazer and cap. For each race the starter must position himself so that every competitor is visible within the narrowest possible field of vision and so that he can be heard clearly by all the athletes.

The starter begins by blowing a whistle to attract the attention of the timekeepers and judges. When the competitors are lined up on the track he brings them to their respective starting marks by giving the order 'On your marks'. In sprint races where starting blocks are used the starter waits for all movement to cease before he raises the starting pistol and gives the additional 'Set' command, after which he holds the athletes in the 'Set' position for a second or so before firing. If some movement occurs or the starter is not happy with the start, he gives the 'Stand up' order and the procedure begins all over again.

If an athlete commits a false start by moving fractionally before the gun fires, either the starter or a recaller fires a second gun to signal to the competitors that the start is

The starter's raised gun is connected to an automatic timing system.

void and must begin again. When this occurs the starter must warn the offending athlete before re-starting the race.

Timekeepers

The timekeepers take up positions level with the finish line on the outside of the track and are usually seated in a tiered stand so that they all have a clear view of the finish.

Using stopwatches or manually-operated electronic timers the timekeepers record the race times for each competitor, starting their watches the instant they see the flash or smoke from the starter's gun and stopping them as each athlete's torso reaches the finish line. The race winner's time has to be recorded by at least three different watches and each timekeeper acts independently, passing his written recording only to the chief timekeeper who must decide the official times for each competitor.

In races of 800 metres or over the timekeepers may also supply intermediate lap times and even kilometre splits.

Lap scorers

These officials position themselves close to the finish line from which point they can more effectively record the number and times of laps covered by each athlete in running and walking races longer than 1500 m. The lap scorers are also required to operate the lap indicator board where available, or else to signal to the competitors how many laps remain after each circuit, ringing a bell (or in the USA firing a gun) to indicate the final lap of the race.

Other officials

Other important officials include the photo-finish judges, who operate the photo-finish equipment when in use, the wind gauge operator and the announcer who communicates, via a public-address system, event results and other relevant information concerning the competitors and events in progress.

100 METRES

Of the wide spectrum of activities which go to make up the sport of athletics, sprinting is undoubtedly the most fundamental. The 100 metres is *the* prestige event among the sprints and, more than for any other sprint race, the successful 100 metres runner requires a combination of fast reactions, leg speed and explosive power: attributes which cannot be readily obtained even through the most modern training techniques. In other words, the champion sprinter is born and not made.

The start for the 100 metres is situated at the opposite end of the homestraight from the finish line in front of the main stand, the athletes lining up immediately behind a scratch line, with each competitor in a separate lane and, as in all sprint events, the standard crouch start off starting blocks is employed. Because the 100 metres is one of the shortest and quickest track events, a good start is essential. A split-second hesitation at the gun could leave a competitor a full metre behind the opposition, greatly reducing his winning chances. Therefore, because tension is always high before a race, nervous athletes often false start.

At the gun the competitors endeavour to get into full stride as quickly as possible, reaching maximum speed at or around the 60 m (197 ft) mark, from which point even the best sprinters begin to slow. In the latter stages of the race the sprinters try to relax and maintain momentum, and will be seen lunging forward (or 'dipping') just before the finish in order to gain a few, often vital, inches over near rivals.

Among the fastest top speeds so far recorded for a male sprinter is one of close to 43 km/h (27 mph) by American Bob Hayes, during a 100 yards (91.44 m) race in 1963. The best women sprinters approach 39 km/h (24 mph). Nowadays, the target for top male sprinters is to run the 100 metres in 10 seconds, although anything faster than 10.40 sec. is of international class. Women sprinters are less powerful and possess a generally shorter stride length than their male counterparts, making them a second slower, on average, over the 100 metres.

By far the highest proportion of the world's male sprinting talent comes from the United States, with black American sprinters very much predominating over their white countrymen at the highest international level. Currently, some 50 per cent of the world's top female sprinters come from the Eastern bloc countries, with the United States, Western Europe and the Commonwealth countries supplying the rest.

Currently there are more female sprinters of good international class in the UK than there are male sprinters.

Opposite above: *Sprinters in the 'set' position a split second before the starter's gun fires.* Left: *The athlete in the foreground holds on to win from the lunging figure on his left.*

Ashford, Evelyn (USA): Born 15.4.1957. The only woman to have consistently beaten the cream of East Germany's world leading female sprinters, she achieved unprecedented 100/200 metres sprint doubles at both the 1979 and 1981 World Cup competitions and also became the Pan-American Games 100 and 200 metres champion in 1979. Despite an altitude-assisted 100 metres world record of 10.79 in 1983, she failed to gain a medal in the sprints at the World Championships, sustaining an injury during the 100 metres final.

Marlies Gohr (GDR)

Gohr, Marlies (GDR): Born 21.3.1958. The first woman to beat 11.00 sec. for 100 metres on fully automatic timing with 10.88 in 1977, she made up for missing out on the 1980 Olympic 100 metres title by 0.01 sec., with a resounding victory in the 100 metres at the inaugural World Championships in 1983. She retained her European Championships 100 metres sprint title in Athens in 1982 and has won four sprint relay gold medals, from two Olympic Games and both the European and World Championships.

Lewis, Carl (USA): Born 1.7.1961. Having first come to prominence as a long jumper without equal (see Long Jump personalities), he carved his niche in the sprinting hall of fame by becoming athletics' first 100 metres world champion in Helsinki in 1983. Already the fastest non-altitude-assisted sprinter on earth, with times of 9.97 and 19.75 sec. for the 100 and 200 metres, respectively, before those Championships, he picked up a third gold medal in Helsinki, anchoring the US 4×100 metres relay team to a new world record of 37.86 sec.

Smith, Calvin (USA): Born 8.1.1961. In 1983 he broke one of the oldest athletics world records in the books, eclipsing the 1968 100 metres mark with 9.93 at the 2,195 m (7,200 ft) altitude of Colorado Springs. The previous year he had run an even faster wind-assisted 9.91 in East Germany at sea level. Previously an inconsistent performer, he excelled at the inaugural World Championships winning the 200 metres, placing second in the 100 metres and sharing in the USA's world record 4 × 100 metres relay victory.

Calvin Smith (USA)

Thomas, Shirley (UK): Born 15.6.1963. A bright sprint prospect for the future, she took the 100 metres silver medal at the 1981 European Junior Championships, clocking 11.43, and added European and World Championship sprint relay silver medals to her collection in 1982 and 1983, respectively. She also showed promise in reaching the World Championships individual 100 metres semi-finals in the latter year.

Wells, Alan (UK): Born 3.5.1952. Having won his first major sprint medals, including the 200 metres gold

(windy 20.12), at the 1978 Commonwealth Games, he quickly consolidated his reputation as both the fastest and most competitive British sprinter ever, achieving numerous UK sprint records at 100 and 200 metres and crowning his meteoric rise to world class with victory in the 100 metres (10.25) at the Moscow Olympics. Following wins at both 100 and 200 metres during the 1982 Brisbane Commonwealth Games, he narrowly failed to gain a medal at either 100 or 200 metres at the World Championships in Helsinki in 1983.

200 METRES

The 200 metres sprint, unlike the 100 metres, starts on a bend, taking in the whole bend and the homestraight, and is exactly half a circuit of the standard 400 metres track. The inclusion of a bend adds extra distance to all but the inside lane, so a staggered start is necessary.

The best 200 metres runners are often equally capable at the shorter sprints but with the longer race, although raw speed is essential, strength plays a greater part. A good 200 metres sprinter has to be able to distribute his effort evenly over the full distance, running equally well on the bend and the straight.

Bend running is, in fact, more difficult than it may appear, for at speed the athlete tends to be forced towards the outside edge of his lane, which marginally increases the running distance. Thus sprinters can be seen to counteract this tendency by leaning towards the lane's inside edge. The competitors on the inside lanes are at an even greater disadvantage than those on the outside, for the bend is tighter on the inside of the track and, therefore, harder to negotiate. The only consolation is that on the bend the runners on the inside can see those on the outside, are thus aware of their relative positions and are better able to pace themselves during the first half of the race. The athletes on the outside are, in effect, 'running blind'.

The stagger unwinds coming off the bend, revealing the true race positions. It is at this point, with the length of the straight still to run, that the athletes must try to avoid losing momentum if they are to stay close enough to the opposition to be able to make good use of a dip finish. They must, therefore, try to maintain relaxed sprinting form, in spite of tightening leg muscles, right through to the finish line.

Top-class sprinters tend to run the second 100 of a 200 metres faster than the first, despite the effects of fatigue, because full speed cannot be employed in bend running and the second 100 has the benefit of a flying start. Good sprinters can, however, achieve the same average speed over 200 metres as they do in the shorter sprint. Male sprinters of the highest international standard often record times of close to

Above: *The sprinter's high knee lift enables him to achieve maximum stride-length at top speed.*

20.00 sec. for the 200 metres. Top UK national level male sprinters expect to clock 21.00 sec. or faster. Top female sprinters run the 200 metres approximately two seconds slower than their male counterparts.

Performances at all sprint distances can be affected by a number of factors. For instance, some track surfaces are more conducive to fast sprint times than others. The weather has a big influence too: cold is detrimental to sprinting performance, whilst strong winds can increase or decrease sprinting speed, depending on the wind's direction.

Altitude can also have an affect on sprint performances. The thinner atmosphere at altitudes of around 2000 m (6560 ft) presents less wind resistance than at sea level, enabling the sprinter to achieve marginally greater speeds.

Cook, Kathy (UK): Born 3.5.1960. A holder of British records at 100 (11.10), 200 (22.13) and 400 metres (50.46), her strongest distance is undoubtedly 200 metres. Her first major victory was in capturing the 1981 World Student Games 200 metres title, but superior performances include her second places in both the European Championships and Commonwealth Games 200 metres in 1982 and her 200 metres third place at the 1983 World Championships. She also won sprint relay gold medals at the Commonwealth Games of 1978 and 1982.

Pietro Mennea (Italy)

Lattany, Mel (USA): Born 10.8.1959. In 1981 he ranked second in the world over 100 (10.04) and 200 metres (20.21) and won both the World Student Games 100 metres and the World Cup 200 metres titles. Following a patchy 1982 season he hit top form in 1983 only to lose a shoe during the vital 200 metres trial race for the American World Championships team. He underlined what he might have achieved in Helsinki by smashing the world figures for 300 metres (32.15) that year.

Mennea, Pietro (Italy): Born 28.6.1952. The most bemedalled of all the world's top sprinters, his greatest achievements include his Olympic 200 metres victory in 1980 and his European Championships wins at 200 (1974 and 1978) and 100 metres (1978). He set an altitude-assisted 200 metres world record (19.72) in 1979 and has maintained consistent world class form over an unprecedented 12-year span. Following a brief period of retirement he captured the 1983 World Championships

200 metres bronze medal, clocking 20.51.

Ottey, Merlene (Jamaica): Born 10.5.1960. One of the most accomplished of Commonwealth-born female sprinters ever, she entered real world class in 1980, placing third in that year's Olympic 200 metres final in 22.20, before going on to capture the 1982 Commonwealth 200 metres title and a silver in the 100. Her finest performance to date came when placing second in the 200 metres (22.19) at the inaugural World Championships, in which she also gained a 4 × 100 metres relay bronze medal.

Merlene Ottey (Jamaica)

Sharp, Cameron (UK): Born 3.6.1958. Emerging from Alan Wells' shadow in 1982 Sharp was selected for the European Championships and against all odds took the 200 metres silver medal, clocking 20.47 behind the winner. At the Commonwealth Games later in the year he won three bronze medals, in the individual 100 and 200 metres (both behind Wells) and the 4 × 100 metres relay, in which he had also picked up a gold at the 1978 Games at Edmonton.

Wockel, Barbel (GDR): Born 21.3.1955. Although not the fastest female over 200 metres (22.01/ 21.85 w) she has certainly been the most competitive, winning every major 200 metres title that she has contested, including both the 1976 and 1980 Olympic titles, the 1982 European title and the European Junior title in 1973. In addition, she has figured in several gold medal winning and world record breaking GDR sprint relay teams and placed second in the 1982 European Championships 100 metres.

400 METRES

The longest and most demanding of the sprints, the 400 metres is an event in which more than just speed and natural ability are required to reach international class. High degrees of strength and stamina, developed through a rigorous training programme, are essential to the champion one-lap runner.

A complete circuit of the standard 400 metres track, the race starts at the beginning of the first bend. A staggered start is called for but the distance between the scratch lines in each lane is double that for the 200 metres sprint, as there are two bends to be negotiated.

Perhaps more than in most track events, pace judgement and distribution of effort are key factors in 400 metres running. The experienced one-lap runner will cover the first half of the race at a little less than top speed, coming within a second or so of his best 200 metres sprint time, whilst keeping something in reserve for the remainder of the race. The runners work hard to maintain their momentum around the second bend as the stagger unwinds and as the field enters the homestraight, the athletes' relative race positions will become clear.

It is often in the final straight that a race is won or lost, since

Good bend-running requires the sprinter to stay close to the lane's inside edge.

some runners will feel the effects of fatigue more than others. In a prolonged sprint such as this, lactic acid builds up in the athletes' leg muscles causing considerable discomfort and slowing forward progress. This 'tying up' in the final stages of the race is sometimes quite dramatic and the winner is usually the person who has run the first 300 metres at a sensible pace and can best maintain stride length and sprinting speed all the way to the tape, perhaps overtaking several athletes who have used up too much energy during the first part of the race. In a well-judged race the winner's second 200 metres will have been no more than 1–2 seconds slower than the first.

Over 400 metres, successful international competitors should be capable of times of 45.50 sec. or faster and 51.00 sec. or faster for men and women, respectively. Athletes in the top flight at UK national level would be expected to produce times in the region of sub 47.00 sec. for men and sub 52.50 sec. for women.

The 400 metres is undoubtedly a race for the specialist, requiring greater stamina than for the pure sprints but greater speed than for the middle distances. Therefore, only a few very exceptional one-lap runners compete with anything like equal success at the 200 or 800 metres.

Bennett, Todd (UK): Born 6.7.1962. A precocious talent as a teenager, he won the European Junior Championships 400 metres title in 1981 clocking 47.18. A year later he placed fifth in the Brisbane Commonwealth Games 400 metres final and picked up gold and silver medals in the 4 × 400 metres relays in Brisbane and at the European Championships the same year. At the World Championships in 1983 he reached the 400 metres semi-finals and shared in the bronze medals as a member of the 4 × 400 metres relay squad.

Bert Cameron (Jamaica)

Cameron, Bert (Jamaica): Born 16.11.1959. Following his Commonwealth 400 metres record of 44.58 in 1981 he soon became the most consistent one-lap runner in the world. His first major successful race was the 1982 Commonwealth Games 400 metres and just one year later he made his mark in athletics history, winning the 400 metres final in 45.05 at the first World Championships to take the gold medal ahead of strong American and West German opposition.

Kocembova, Tatyana (Czechoslovakia): Born 2.5.1962. Perhaps inspired

by her illustrious team mate, Jarmila Kratochvilova, she suddenly made a dramatic improvement in 1983, becoming the world's third fastest female 400 metres runner with her 48.59 in second place in the World Championships final, before earning another silver medal with the Czech 4 × 400 metres relay team. She capped her 1983 season with an individual 400 metres win and a leg in the Czech's long relay victory during the European Cup final.

Koch, Marita (GDR): Born 18.2.1957. The world's leading female 400 metres runner

Marita Koch (GDR)

Scutt, Michelle (UK): Born 17.6.1960. Good enough to reach the 400 metres semi-finals and share in the British quartet's third place in the 4 × 400 metres relay final at the 1980 Olympic Games, she had an even better year in 1982. That year she set a Commonwealth and UK 400 metres record of 50.63 and went on to take the 400 metres silver medal at the Commonwealth Games at Brisbane.

Weber, Hartmut (FRG): Born 17.10.1960. Following his 1979 European Junior Championships 400 metres title and a 400 metres win in the 1981 European Cup final, he added the Senior European one-lap title to his collection in 1982, clocking 44.72, and helped the West German squad to a set of gold medals in the 4 × 400 metres relay at those championships. A leading European contender for the World Championships 400 metres title in 1983, he could finish only fifth in that event but anchored the West German team to second place in the 4 × 400 metres relay and later notched up his second European Cup final 400 metres victory.

for several years, she became Olympic 400 metres champion in 1980 and two years later retained her European Championships 400 metres title in Athens. In addition to a share in two GDR European Championships 4 × 400 metres victories (1978 and 1982) she had set six world records at 400 metres (49.19 to 48.15) and three at 200 metres (22.06 to 21.71) up to the end of 1983. Concentrating on the short sprints at the World Championships in 1983, she won the 200 metres and placed second in the 100 before contributing to the GDR's 4 × 100 and 4 × 400 metres relay wins.

800 METRES

The runners break for the inside lane at the beginning of the backstraight in an 800 metres race.

Run over two full laps of the track, the 800 metres is considered to be a middle distance event, although at international level the race is virtually a prolonged sprint. The 800 metres runner requires a combination of speed, strength and stamina and tends to be less heavily muscled than are many sprinters, since explosive sprinting power is not quite so essential to the middle distance athlete.

The race starts at the beginning of the first bend, runners adopting a standing start position, as in all track events longer than the sprints. In all major races at this distance the athletes run the first 100 m in lanes, necessitating a staggered start, to avoid the possibility of collisions during the initial sprint. The use of lanes limits the field to 8 runners (9 on one of the few 9-lane tracks) in a championship event, but at less significant meetings, some lanes may be shared by two runners, increasing the field to 10 or 11 competitors at most. The point at which the field may break from lanes is indicated by red flags situated on either side of the track at the beginning of the backstraight.

The runner in pole position (pacemaker) during the race dictates the pace for the rest of the field and unless that athlete is confident of being able to outrun the opposition in the later stages of the race, he will ensure that the first lap is run at a brisk pace. As the runners pass the finish line to complete the first lap, the bell (or gun) sounds to signal the final circuit and the time at 400 m is announced. If the race is to result in a fast time it is crucial that a good pace is maintained for the next half lap, as this is the make-or-break stage of the race as far as record attempts are concerned. The race leader may also employ a fast-pace tactic to try to tire the known fast finishers in the field, before they can use their

sprinting speed in the latter stages of the race. Some athletes may be seen to sprint (or 'kick') away from the field at the beginning of the last bend, particularly if the early pace has been slow. However, if the race has been fast throughout there is likely to be a frantic mass sprint finish down the homestraight, with the fleetest athlete prevailing over his rivals.

In a major race at this relatively short distance there is little time to rectify tactical errors, so a potential race winner has to stay close to the leader and avoid getting boxed in, i.e. becoming trapped on the inside lane by runners immediately in front and alongside. Any athlete more than a few strides behind the leaders on the last lap would find it extremely difficult to make up lost ground, particularly against international-class opposition. In a fast race the first lap is invariably quicker than the second.

Times of 1 min. 46.0 sec., or faster, are regularly recorded by top international male runners and at UK national level times of 1:48.0, or faster, are quite common. Women of comparable standard are 12–14 seconds slower than the men.

It is not uncommon for 800 metre-type athletes to achieve good results at 1500 metres and the mile, even though the two-lap race is quite a specialized event.

Coe, Sebastian (UK): Born 29.9.1956. His 800 metres world record of 1:41.73, set in 1981, must rank as one of the outstanding performances ever achieved in the history of athletics, being a phenomenal 1.71 seconds faster than the next best performer on record. However, he had failed to win an Olympic or European 800 metres title despite three attempts between 1978 and 1982, although he became Olympic 1500 metres champion in 1980 and four times set mile/1500 metres world records up to the end of 1982. Glandular fever ruled him out of the World Championships in 1983.

Druppers, Rob (Netherlands): Born 29.4.1962. Within one year of failing to get through his 800 metres heat at the 1981 European Junior Championships, he was third fastest in the world over two laps (1:44.54) in 1982 and placed fifth in the European Championships 800 metres final. His outstanding potential was dramatically demonstrated during the 1983 World Championships, when he took the 800 metres silver medal, clocking a Dutch record of 1:44.20.

Kratochvilova, Jarmila (Czechoslovakia): Born 26.1.1951. Second only to Marita Koch over 400 metres up to the end of 1982, with Olympic (1980) and European (1982) silver medals and a 1981 World Cup victory to her name, she switched to 800 metres in 1983 with devastating results. Setting a phenomenal 800 metres world record of 1:53.28 in only her third serious race over the distance, she went on to win the World Championships 800 metres title, at the age of 32, and also picked up the 400 metres gold medal in world record time (47.99) in Koch's absence.

McDermott, Kirsty (UK): Born 6.8.1962. A poor fourth place in the WAAA Championships 800 metres final in 1982 didn't auger well for her medal chances at that year's Commonwealth Games, but a Welsh 800 metres record of 2:00.56 just before the games seemed to point to something special in Brisbane. Sure enough, she won the 800 metres to become Wales' first female representative to win a Commonwealth Games athletics gold medal.

Jarmila Kratochvilova (Czech)

Sebastian Coe (UK)

Mineyeva, Olga (USSR): Born 1.10.1952. Overshadowed by her record-breaking countrywoman Nadezhda Olizarenko in the 1980 Olympic women's 800 metres final, in which she placed second in a faster time (1:54.81) than the previous world record, Mineyeva made no mistake at the European Championships in Athens two years later. There she won the 800 metres in convincing style clocking a fast 1:55.41. Nowadays, with the quick turnover of world-class female middle distance runners, it is rare for a girl to win medals at more than one major championships.

Wulbeck, Willi (FRG): Born 18.12.1954. Ten years after placing second, behind Steve Ovett, in the 800 metres at the 1973 European Junior Championships, he finally came good to capture the most prestigious 800 metres title available, in his fastest time (1:43.65), at the 1983 World Championships. Prior to Helsinki his finest achievements included fourth place in the 1976 Olympic 800 metres final, a European Cup two-lap win in 1977 and no less than 10 FRG 800 metres titles.

1500 METRES AND THE MILE

The mile and the 1500 metres (or 'metric mile') are among the most popular of all athletics events. The name of the most famous miler of all, Dr Roger Bannister, the man who made athletics history in 1954 by running the first ever sub 4 minute mile, is known to sports fans the world over. Some 30 years on the men's mile world record is well under 3 min. 50 sec. and the sub 4 minute mile is a common achievement, with literally hundreds of different athletes having since breached this once magical barrier.

Although the mile is not a major championship event, as is the 1500 metres, it is still recognized for world record purposes by the IAAF and is often included on the programmes of national and international athletics meetings, particularly in Britain and the USA.

Equivalent to just over 1609 m, the mile is a little longer than four laps of a standard metric track, starting from a curved scratch line, 9.35 m (31 ft) from the finish line, on the homestraight. The 1500 metres is run over 3¾ laps of a 400 m track and starts at the beginning of the backstraight.

Nowadays, fast times seem to be of paramount importance in middle distance races, so meeting organizers often arrange for a pacemaker (known as the 'hare' or 'rabbit') to lay on a

To ensure a good position in the latter stages of a mile or 1500 metres race the runners must stay close to the leader right from the gun.

fast early pace in many non-championship mile/1500 metres events, a practice which is frowned upon by the IAAF. The pacemaker will take the lead right from the gun, averaging well under 60 sec. per lap in a men's race and 65 sec. for a women's, in an international class event, for at least two laps. The 'hare' does not run to win but, more likely, jogs the last couple of laps once the pacemaking task is completed.

In a 1500 metres race the intermediate times announced relate to each 400 m lap but for a mile these times generally relate to each quarter mile. The exact point at which each quarter mile finishes (this varies from lap to lap since 400 m is equivalent to only 437.14 yards) is indicated by an official who stands level with the exact spot as the runners approach, so that accurate times can be taken for each lap the instant the runner passes him.

If the initial pace is slow the field will remain closely bunched together for much of the way but at the bell the race will spring to life, as the leading runners are sure to launch their finishing kicks at the start of the last lap, or certainly no later than with 200 m (218.57 yds) to go. Any athlete careless enough to get boxed in approaching the bell is unlikely to win, for during the last lap the runners behind will stream past on the outside, leaving the trapped athlete well behind and out of contention.

Final laps of faster than 54.0 sec. for men and 60.0 sec. for women are not uncommon in slow tactical mile/1500 metres races of international class. In a fast race, in which a record is under fire, a runner may break away from the field with as much as a lap and a half to go but the final circuit will not be as fast as in a tactical race, in view of the initial pace. Although slow tactical races are more common in major championships—since on these occasions winning medals takes priority over fast times—they are confined almost exclusively to men's races for in women's major middle distance races the pace is generally fast throughout, the gold medal winners regularly setting championship records. On the whole, the first and last laps of a mile/1500 metres race are the quickest, regardless of race tactics, as the competitors tend to run hard from the gun to gain a good position on the first circuit, whilst a sprint finish on the last lap is inevitable.

Although the world's finest male middle distance runners hail from every corner of the globe, on the women's side the greatest strength in depth is concentrated in the Eastern bloc countries (particularly the GDR and USSR), which nowadays provide virtually all the 800 and 1500 metres medallists at major championships.

Top international-class male middle distance runners will regularly clock sub 3 min. 38 sec. 1500 metres timings, whilst performances of better than 3:42.0 are quite commonplace at UK national level. A 3:42.0 1500 metres is approximately equivalent to a 4 minute mile, the 18 seconds time difference being the estimated running time for the additional 120 yards of a mile race at 4 minute miling pace. The mile is seemingly less popular with the women and, subsequently, mile times lag far behind those for 1500 metres. Internationally, women run many more sub 4:00.0 metric miles (worth 4:19/4:20 for a mile) than sub 4:25.0 miles. Good class times at national level are anything faster than 4:10 m/4:35 y.

Few middle distance runners cover enough mileage in training to excel at races longer than 3 km (2 miles), although it is quite common for 1500 m/mile athletes to progress to the longer distances later in their running careers.

Approaching the bell for the final lap the athlete wearing number 58 and the runner just behind him are completely boxed in. In this position their winning chances are virtually nil, for they are unable to follow the runners on the outside who are moving to the front of the field ready to launch a last lap sprint finish.

Steve Cram (UK)

Cram, Steve (UK): Born 14.10.1960. A 3:57.4 miler and Commonwealth Games competitor at the age of 17, he reached the 1980 Olympic 1500 metres final at 19 and at 20 became the youngest ever sub-3:50 miler (3:49.95). In 1982 he captured both European and Commonwealth 1500 metres titles and the following year, while still only 22, beat all the world's top milers, bar Seb Coe, to become world 1500 metres champion and complete another chapter in a career which already qualifies him as one of the greatest milers ever.

Boxer, Christina (UK): Born 25.3.1957. In 1979 she set a UK mile record of 4:30.2 and became the first British woman to break 2 minutes for 800 metres (1:59.05). A winner of several national 800/1500 metres titles, she had to wait until 1982 to win her first major international title, winning the 1500 metres (4:08.28) at the Commonwealth Games. She also reached the 1980 Olympic 800 metres semi-finals and the 1500 metres final at the 1983 World Championships.

Decker, Mary (USA): Born 4.8.1958. The world's fastest 880 yards runner indoors at the age of 15, she bounced back after several years of injury to win the 1979 Pan-American Games 1500 metres title and set women's indoor and outdoor mile bests of 4:17.55 and 4:21.7, respectively, in 1980. Following further injury in 1981 she regained the mile world record (4:18.08) in 1982 and the very next year defeated the cream of the USSR's female middle distance runners to take the 1500 metres gold medal at the World Championships.

Kazankina, Tatyana (USSR): Born 17.12.1951. The greatest middle distance runner that the Soviet Union has yet produced, she won the 800/1500 metres double at the 1976 Olympic Games and retained the latter title four years later in Moscow. Of her four world records at 800/1500 metres her last mark of 3:52.4 at the longer distance represents one of the finest performances in athletics history. Moving up in distance she placed third over 3000 metres at the 1983 World Championships.

Tatyana Kazankina (USSR)

Ovett, Steve (UK): Born 9.10.1955. Indisputably the world's No. 1 miler between June 1977 and July 1980, he won all 45 of his 1500 m/mile races during that period. The European Junior 800 metres champion back in 1973, he gained the European 1500 metres title in 1978 and the Olympic 800 metres title two years later. After a long period of injury in 1982, he set a 1500 metres world record of 3:30.77 in 1983 (his fourth mile/1500 metres record) after having run an uncharacteristically poor tactical race at that year's World Championships to finish only fourth.

Scott, Steve (USA): Born 5.5.1956. The first American to run a sub-3:50 mile and the last man to beat Steve Ovett in a mile/1500 metres race before the Briton began his record unbeaten run, Scott has posed the biggest threat to British miling supremacy in recent years. The US's finest miling talent since the great Jim Ryun, he ran the second fastest ever mile of 3:47.69 in 1982 and took the 1500 metres silver medal at the 1983 World Championships to achieve his finest international success to date.

5000/10,000 METRES AND WOMEN'S 3000 METRES

The long distance track events attract a breed of athlete whose running ability is best suited to the particular tactical requirements of the longer races, which are in many ways unlike those of the middle distances. For instance, because of the much greater training mileages clocked up by long distance athletes, they tend not to carry any excess body-weight and are, therefore, generally of lighter build than the average middle distance runner. Distance athletes still need to be strong, however, possessing great reserves of stamina and, surprisingly, a fair turn of speed if they are to have any chance of victory on the last lap of a close race.

The 3000 metres is currently the longest major champion-ship track event for women, the 5000 and 10,000 metres having only recently gained official recognition and world record status as women's events. In contrast, men's 5000 and 10,000 metres races have been staged at the Olympic Games since 1912. The runners start from a curved scratch line at all three distances, the 3000 ($7\frac{1}{2}$ laps) and 5000 metres ($12\frac{1}{2}$ laps) both commencing at the 200 m mark and the 10,000 metres (25 laps) starting at the beginning of the first bend.

The fields for long distance races are generally much larger than for the middle distance events, as there is little danger of

runners tripping over each other at the relatively slower pace. After a fairly brisk opening lap the pace settles down to a more or less constant speed, the procession of runners spread along maybe 20 m (66 ft) of the track in the early stages. It is not so important for runners to stay close to the race leaders, at least in the early stages of a distance race, as there is plenty of time to make up lost ground. A 'hare' might be included in a long distance race to ensure a fast early pace but in the past relatively few distance records have resulted from deliberately-paced record attempts.

During a race times are usually announced for each kilometre ($2\frac{1}{2}$ laps) or even for individual laps, but more important, particularly in major races, a lap indicator board, or an electronic lap indicator, is placed near the finish line to show the runners how many laps remain after each circuit. The average lap times for an international men's 5000 metres race would be in the region of 63–65 sec. and for 10,000 metres, around 66–67 sec. Over the same distances top female internationals would average around 10 sec. per lap slower than the men. Top female 3000 metres runners lap at around 69–70 sec.

As the race progresses it will be seen that a number of different runners take it in turns to lead. Very rarely does one athlete lead for most or all of a distance race, for the pacemaker has the difficult and tiring task of dictating the pace and acting as a windbreak for those behind. The athlete who leads for a

The indicator board shows 25 laps to go as the line of runners converges on the inside lane at the start of a gruelling 10,000 metres race.

prolonged period will invariably be passed by fresher rivals in the final stages, although there have been a few exceptional athletes capable of literally running away from the opposition during the race.

The potential race winners, or medallists, begin to sort themselves out from perhaps the halfway mark as some athletes begin to lose contact with the main field, leaving the strongest and freshest athletes in the leading group. From this point the slower runners can start to become a problem, for even in international distance races the back markers will, sooner or later, be lapped by the leaders. Where these trailing runners have the courtesy to move out into the second or third lanes to allow the leaders to pass there is no problem but, often, offending runners will not move out, forcing the leaders to weave in and out to avoid the stragglers.

In the last few laps of a race, when the runners are becoming increasingly tired, various tactical ploys may be seen to be used. An habitual front runner may try to break the opposition by surging (i.e. continually speeding up and slowing down the pace), which is designed to disrupt the other runners' rhythm and concentration, sapping their stamina and, hopefully, forcing them to give up the chase. Alternatively, one competitor may put in a prolonged burst of speed over a full lap or more in order to make a decisive break which will clinch the race. Where no individual athlete is sufficiently confident to try for a decisive break the race will probably be decided in a last-lap sprint. Even in a fast 10,000 metres race the leaders will display a fair turn of finishing speed but in a slow race the last lap burn up can be breathtaking. Some international long distance runners have produced finishing kicks which would not disgrace a world class miler, times such as sub 55.0 sec. (men) and sub 61.0 sec. (women) having been clocked for the last 400 m of a race. Whoever wins, the spectator can be sure that the smoothest striding and most relaxed looking runners in the last few laps will be there or thereabouts at the finish.

As in the middle distance events, the majority of the world's top female international long distance runners come from the Eastern bloc countries, whereas the cream of the male distance athletes are quite evenly distributed over the continents.

A guide to the level of performances which could be expected of top international and UK national athletes at the standard long distance track events is given in the following chart:

International standard	Men	Women
3000 metres	—	sub 8:55.0
5000 metres	sub 13:25.0	sub 15:30.0
10,000 metres	sub 28:10.0	sub 32:40.0
UK national standard		
3000 metres	—	sub 9:15.0
5000 metres	sub 13:40.0	sub 16:30.0
10,000 metres	sub 28:40.0	sub 34:30.0

It must be remembered that the women's 5000 and 10,000 metres events are very much undeveloped and, therefore, national and international standards in these events are likely to improve quite dramatically within the next few years.

In a distance race as long as the women's 3000 metres event the runners must try to maintain an even pace throughout to conserve energy, whilst watching for any sudden breaks.

Coghlan, Eamonn (Eire): Born 24.11.1952. One of Ireland's finest ever middle/long distance runners, he seemed destined never to win a major title, placing fourth at the 1976 Olympics and second at the 1978 European Championships over 1500 metres. Over 5000 metres he again finished fourth, at the Moscow Olympics, but achieved a significant victory at that distance in the 1981 World Cup. In 1983 he set a world indoor mile best of 3:49.78 and, for once, maintained his form right through to the World Championships, winning the 5000 metres with consummate ease in 13:28.53.

Alberto Cova (Italy)

Cova, Alberto (Italy): Born 1.12.1958. Following a relatively undistinguished career he produced an astonishing sprint finish during the 10 km at the 1982 European Championships to gain an unexpected victory. He employed identical tactics on the last lap of the World Championships 10 km final the year after and again won the race on the line, clocking 28:01.04. The bubble finally burst during the 1983 European Cup final where he left his sprint finish too late losing again over 10 km.

Mary Decker (USA)

Decker, Mary (USA): Born 4.8.1958. Having previously only dabbled at the longer distances she began rewriting the record books in 1982, setting 5 km (15:08.26) and 10 km (31:35.3) world records and becoming the second woman to run under $8\frac{1}{2}$ minutes (8:29.71) for 3000 metres. At the 1983 World Championships she took on the previously invincible Russians over 3000 metres and beat them convincingly, before repeating the dose over 1500 metres (see Mile/1500 metres: Personalities).

Moorcroft, David (UK): Born 10.4.1953. One of the most underrated of all world-class distance runners, he finally gained just recognition, at the age of 29, when he smashed the 5000 metres world record (clocking 13:00.41) by a huge 5.79 seconds margin to achieve one of the most remarkable performances ever. Surprisingly, he finished only third in the European Championships 5000 metres (13:30.42) that year but won the gold medal in the same event at the Commonwealth Games some weeks later. Originally a miler, he was Commonwealth 1500 metres champion in 1978 and placed third in the European Championships 1500 metres the same season.

Sly, Wendy (UK): Born 5.11.1959. Is primarily responsible for ending the recent decline in British women's middle distance standards. She first approached real world class in 1982, taking second place in the Commonwealth Games women's 3000 metres and setting a Commonwealth record of 8:46.01 for that distance. Her big breakthrough came at the inaugural World Championships where she placed fifth at both 3000 and 1500 metres, clocking a superb 8:37.06 at 1500 m.

Ulmasova, Svetlana (USSR): Born 4.2.1953. The world's leading women's 3000 metres runner for several years, she finally broke the 6-year-old world record in 1982 recording 8:26.78. In addition to a World Cup 3000 metres win in 1979, she became the first woman to retain a European Championships 3000 metres title with her second win in Athens in 1982. Although favourite to win the 1983 World Championships 3000 metres title, she could finish only fourth.

THE MARATHON

Despite the fact that it is one of the toughest long distance running events of all, the marathon is fast becoming one of the most popular athletics activities—for spectators and participants alike.

Dating back to just before the turn of the century, and traditionally the event that the distance runner turned to if he lacked the basic speed to be successful at distances such as 5000 and 10,000 metres, in more recent years the marathon's image has changed dramatically. No longer the event for the 'plodder', the international marathon runner needs the basic speed of the track athlete combined with boundless reserves of stamina and strength. During the last decade the marathon has also become the target of the jogger, the casual fun-runner and just about everybody else, from the seasoned international to the housewife who had only ever run to catch a bus before 'marathon mania' hit the civilized world.

The marathon boom really began with the New York City Marathon, first staged in 1970 and attracting a field of 126 runners. The race first captured the general public's interest in 1976 when the course was changed to take in all five boroughs of the city, which allowed many more spectators to watch the race. By 1977 sufficient runners had been stricken with 'marathon mania' to swell the New York field to 4823: the largest marathon field ever assembled. That number had grown, just four years later, to a phenomenal 14,496 men and women, many of whom were running their first ever marathon.

When 'marathon mania' finally struck Britain it spread like wildfire. In only the second year of its existence, 1982, the London Marathon surpassed even the New York City race in the sheer size of the field taking part, with 16,350 runners starting the race. Like the majority of marathons, outside of the major international championship races, the London Marathon is run on a point-to-point course on roads and, in fact, the odd standard marathon distance of 26 miles 385 yards (42,195 m) is a legacy of the first full marathon to at least finish in London, the 1908 London Olympic marathon.

Mass marathons attract international-class competitors as well as fun-runners but the bulk of the participants usually cover the distance in good—though far from top class—times

The refreshment stations at intervals along the marathon route often present something of a free-for-all, particularly in mass marathons, as runners jockey for positions to try to grab a drink as they run past.

of around three or even four hours. Nowadays, such is the standard of marathon running at international level, that top male competitors must be capable of averaging very close to five minute miling pace (i.e. 2 h. 11 min. 6 sec. overall) for the full marathon distance, whilst the top women must aim for around six minute miling pace (i.e. 2 h. 37 min. 19 sec.). Major international marathons, such as the European Championships, Olympic and Commonwealth Games races, are open only to international athletes and are invariably run on out-and-back courses, usually starting and finishing on a stadium track.

The gruelling nature of the marathon can create serious problems for even the fittest and most experienced long distance runners if they do not take the necessary precautions. The most potentially dangerous hazards of marathon running are dehydration, through profuse sweating, and overheating (hyperthermia) in warm weather. The simplest way for the athlete to counteract these dangers is to drink plenty of liquid during a race and for this purpose refreshment stations are situated at 5 km (approx. 3 mile) intervals along the courses of all major marathon races (1 mile intervals in many mass marathons). However, even drinking regularly throughout a race does not prevent an athlete from sweating away several pounds in bodyweight during a marathon.

Apart from the occasional and relatively minor irritation of blistered feet, the marathon runner's other main concern is fatigue. Obviously, the fitter the runner the better he is able to cope with the effects of fatigue but, regardless of the athlete's physical condition, there comes a point during a marathon—usually around the 18–22 mile (29–35 km) mark—when the runner's muscles have burned up all the available carbohydrate energy source. The body then has to switch over to fat metabolism to provide energy and this transition can cause extreme discomfort, often slowing a runner's progress in the last few miles of the race. This effect is known as 'hitting the wall'. The athlete's only defence against this is to increase his dietary carbohydrate intake (carbohydrate-loading diet) a few days before running a marathon, so as to build up the carbohydrate energy source in the body, thereby delaying the transition to fat metabolism for as long as possible during the race.

The spectator will see no complex tactics in an event such as the marathon. The distance is too long for the sort of energy-sapping bursts of speed and surges employed in track races, so a potential race winner has to either lay on a fast even pace throughout, in the hope of outrunning the opposition, or else he must bide his time and try to make a decisive break in the latter stages of the race. An athlete who takes the lead too early on risks being caught in the last few miles by fresher runners who have distributed their effort more evenly. A hilly course generally favours the particularly strong runners and on such a course the decisive break will often begin at the foot of a steep hill.

Female long distance runners have made astonishing progress in the marathon in recent years, the top girls now running times which would have won medals in men's major international marathons, including the Olympic marathon, as recently as 30 years ago. The indications are that in some ways women are perhaps better suited to marathon running

The moment that every top-class marathon runner must dream of: striding along the final stretch of the course in splendid isolation to breast the tape first and win the race in a world class time.

than men. The transition to fat metabolism in the female body is apparently far less traumatic than in men and at the end of a mass marathon such as the London, women are invariably conspicuous by their absence from the first-aid area. However, it was not until the 1982 European Championships and 1983 World Championships that the first women's major championship marathons were staged and in 1984 Los Angeles will be the venue for the first women's Olympic marathon.

There are no official records for the marathon as different courses can vary quite considerably, from undulating and hilly to flat and fast. Britain has always had a fine tradition in marathon running although up to now, an Olympic marathon title has still not fallen to a British athlete. Even so, many UK marathoners reach international class, a good number of the top male athletes running times of inside 2 h. 16 min., whilst their female counterparts have made sub 2 h. 50 min. clockings quite commonplace.

Rob de Castella (Australia)

Benoit, Joan (USA): Born 16.3.1957. Already the third fastest woman marathoner at the end of 1982 (2:26:11), she produced an astonishing run in the 1983 Boston race smashing the previous women's world best by 2 min. 47 sec. with 2:22:43, which would have won the gold medal in the *men's* marathon at the 1956 Olympic Games! Her first record-breaking exploit occurred in 1981 when she ran a world best of 1:26:21 for 25 km on the road.

de Castella, Rob (Australia): Born 27.12.1957. After running the second fastest marathon ever of 2:08:18 in the 1981 Fukuoka marathon in Japan, he quickly established himself as one of the strongest and most consistent marathon runners in the world. He was a convincing winner of the Commonwealth Games marathon in 1982 and early the next year beat the world's fastest and previously undefeated American marathon star, Alberto Salazar, in the Rotterdam marathon. A resounding 2:10:03 victory in the World Championships race that year confirmed his position as the new world No. 1 marathon man.

Jones, Hugh (UK): Born 1.11.1955. One of the most promising British marathon runners in recent years he first showed his true potential in finishing third in the 1981 New York marathon. Early in 1982 he clocked a best of 2:10:41 in the Tokyo marathon and followed that up with his greatest win to date in the London marathon which he completed in 2:09:24 for a three-minutes victory margin and the fastest time recorded in Britain. Recovering from a long bout of injury he still achieved an excellent eighth place in the 1983 World Championships.

Salazar, Alberto (USA): Born 7.8.1958. He astounded the athletics world in 1980 with a 2:09:41 victory in the New York marathon in his debut at the distance and the following year won the race again in the fastest marathon time ever of 2:08:13. He achieved victory in both the New York and Boston marathons in 1982 but suffered his first defeat in the 1983 Rotterdam race. In addition to his marathon successes he can also be credited with setting up superb American 5 km (13:11:93) and 10 km (27:25:61) track records during 1982.

Smith, Joyce (UK): Born 26.10.1937. An international track athlete since 1956, with a 1974 European Championships 3000 metres bronze medal to her credit, she finally turned to the marathon in 1979. She set six British women's marathon bests in all, her finest performances coming in the 1981 and 1982 London marathons, in the first of which she achieved her first sub-2½ hours clocking (2:29:57). Her UK best is 2:29:43 (1982). At the 1983 World Championships she finished ninth in the marathon at the age of 45.

Waitz, Grete (Norway): Born 1.10.1953. The greatest female marathon runner to date she crowned a brilliant career with victory in the inaugural World Championship women's marathon in 1983. The first woman to run a sub-2½ hour marathon (2:27:33 in 1979) the Norwegian had set four marathon world bests by the time she was 30. She can also point to five world cross-country titles, European Championships bronze medals at 1500 (1974) and 3000 metres (1978), a World Cup 3000 metres victory (1977) and two 3000 metres world records.

Grete Waitz (Norway)

WALKING EVENTS

Race walking is very much the poor relation of the more diverse running, jumping and throwing events in the sport of athletics. This relative unpopularity is mainly due to the fact that race walking is the least spectacular branch of athletics and must appear to the casual observer as rather an unnatural activity.

The most conspicuous aspect of the race walker's style is the exaggerated hip movement which is employed to extend considerably the athlete's stride length, thereby increasing his speed. However, a major criticism of the walking events concerns the official definition of what exactly constitutes walking. The IAAF defines walking as 'progression by steps so taken that unbroken contact with the ground is maintained, i.e. the advancing foot must make contact with the ground before the rear foot leaves the ground'. The rules also stipulate that the leg must be momentarily straightened at the knee during each stride. Judges are always on hand at race walking events to ensure that the rules are closely adhered to but with top walkers reaching speeds of around 14 km/h (9 mph), it is virtually impossible for the naked eye to detect when a walker is breaking contact with the ground (termed 'lifting'). This problem, has, on occasion, threatened the very existence of the sport of race walking.

Race walking is staged both on the track and road, although only performances set on the track are recognized for world record purposes by the IAAF. Of the wide range of men's walking events (1500 m to 50 km) only the 20 km and 50 km road walks are on the Olympic programme, the latter distance being the longest Olympic event. Like the marathon, major international championship walking races invariably start and finish on the stadium track, the greater part of the race taking place on roads outside the stadium. Walkers are just as prone to the effects of heat and dehydration as are long distance runners and, therefore, refreshment stations are provided at 5 km (3 mile) intervals in all walking events of 20 km or over.

The most popular men's track walks are at distances of 3 and 10 km and often serve as national championship races.

Race walking for women is a relatively new branch of athletics but is gaining in popularity. Track races of 3 and 5 km are the most regularly staged women's walking events although, as yet, the IAAF recognises only women's performances over 5 and 10 km for world record purposes. A women's 10,000 metres road walk is to be included in the European Championships athletics programme for the first time in 1986. Inadequate judging in many countries has resulted in the widespread use of highly suspect walking styles, causing a rapid upsurge in international standards in recent years, which Britain has not matched.

Today's top international male walkers need to be capable of times faster than 1 h. 25 min. for 20 km and 4 h. 00 min. for 50 km, whereas UK athletes are considered to be of the highest national standard if capable of times inside 1:33 (20 km) and 4:25 (50 km). The top British female walkers are much closer to the fast improving women's international standards, with a number of UK athletes producing international calibre performances such as sub 14 min. 20 sec. for 3 km and sub 25 min. 00 sec. for 5 km.

International race walking had been an Eastern bloc stronghold for some years until an illustrious band of Mexican walkers came on the scene in the 1970s and virtually rewrote the record books.

Demonstrating perfect style the walker lifts his right foot off the ground only after the left has made solid contact.

Barry, Steve (UK): Born 25.10.1950. The first British walker to approach true world class in almost a decade, he captured the Commonwealth Games 30 km title, ahead of a strong international field, in a fast time of 2 h. 10 min. 16 sec. in 1982. He also set UK track records at 20 km (1:26:22.0) and 10 km (41:13.62) in 1981 and 1982, respectively. A super-fast 20 km road walk of 1:22:51 early in 1983 suggested great things at the World Championships but injury eventually ruled him out of the reckoning.

Canto, Ernesto (Mexico): Born 18.10.1959. Continuing Mexico's fine tradition in race walking, he captured the 20 km title at the 1983 World Championships at the age of 23 and quickly followed that with a second win, over the same distance, at the Pan-American Games. One of the first walkers to clock sub-1 h. 20 min. for 20 km (1:19:02 in 1980) he won his first major event, the Lugano Trophy (race walking World Cup) 20 km event in 1981.

Cook, Sue (Australia): Born 20.8.1956. A prolific record breaker, she has set world marks on the track at 1 mile (6:47.9 in 1981), 3 km

Sue Cook (Australia)

(12:56.57, 1982), 5 km (22:32.4, 1982) and 10 km (46:42.6, 1982). That 10 km time would have been good enough to take the bronze medal in the *men's* race at the European Championships of 1950 and her world 20 km road best of 1:41:41.6 is another exceptional performance.

José Marin (Spain)

Marin, José (Spain): Born 21.1.1950. One of relatively few world-class Spanish athletes, he made his name in 1982 becoming the European 20 km champion and 50 km silver medallist within three days. Again displaying superb form at the World Championships the following year, he placed second in the 50 km event and narrowly failed to take the bronze medal in the 20 km. On the track he set world records for 2 hours (28,165 metres) and 30 km (2 h. 8 min. 00 sec.) in 1979.

Tyson, Carol (UK): Born 15.12.1957. One of the more recent pioneers of women's race walking, she set world marks on the track at 3 km (13:25.2) and 5 km (23:11.2) in 1979 whilst only 21. In addition to several WAAA titles at 5 and 10 km she also still holds the unofficial UK record for the mile walk (7:14.3), which she set during a 3 km race back in 1977 when still only 19.

Weigel, Ronald (GDR): Born 8.8.1950. A relatively undistinguished career, since his second place in the 1977 European Junior Championships 10 km and a world best indoor 20 km (1:20:40) in 1980, was dramatically transformed at the 1983 World Championships when he achieved a decisive victory in the 50 km event. His winning time of 3 h. 43 min. 08 sec., some $3\frac{1}{2}$ min. clear of the silver medallist, was the fastest yet recorded in a major international championship.

RELAYS

The relays are races between teams of four athletes, each of whom runs a quarter of the total race distance. Both the 4 × 100 and 4 × 400 metres relays are major international championship events, for men and women, and are traditionally the very last races on the meeting programme, serving as an exciting grand finale.

All relays have a staggered start but only the lead-off runner uses starting blocks. Having run the first stage (or leg), the lead-off runner passes a plastic baton 30 cm (12 in) long and weighing approximately 50 g (1¾ oz) to his team's second-leg runner, who in turn passes it on until the athlete on the last (anchor) leg receives the baton and carries it through the finish. Only the athlete who drops a baton may retrieve it, if he is to continue the race and avoid the entire team's disqualification. The actual baton passing (the changeover) has to be accomplished within a designated 20 m (66 ft) long changeover zone. These zones are marked by boundary lines in each lane. A changeover executed outside of a zone results in the offending team's disqualification.

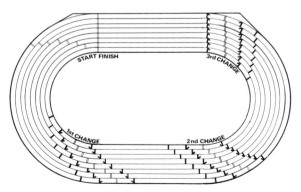

Standard track showing the staggered start, changeover zones (indicated by hooked lines) and acceleration zones for the 4 × 100 metres relay.

Fast, efficient baton passing, particularly in the 4 × 100 metres event, is the key to successful relay running. Often the team which, on paper, boasts the fastest individual athletes will be beaten by the one which displays superior baton passing.

4 × 100 metres relay: Basically a flat-out sprint, the 4 × 100 metres relay covers one complete lap and the entire race is run in lanes. The four legs are divided by scratch lines marked in each lane at 100 m, 200 m and 300 m distances from the finish and the three changeover zones extend 10 m (33 ft) either side of these scratch lines. The athletes on legs 2 to 4 start from a line situated 10 m before each changeover zone, which denotes the beginning of an acceleration zone, used by the sprinters to build up speed prior to entering the changeover zone.

As the second-leg runner enters the changeover zone the lead-off runner should by then be close enough to be able to pass the baton forward, usually from his right hand, into the upturned palm of the outgoing runner's left hand (known as the 'downsweep' technique), taking care not to trip him from behind. The remaining changeovers are also alternated in this way, so that the anchor leg runner receives the baton in his

In the 4 × 100 metres relay the baton changeover is crucial. Here the athletes are using the upsweep style, the incoming runner swinging the baton up into her partner's hand.

left hand. Another popular changeover method, known as the 'upsweep' technique, is when the baton is passed upwards into the outgoing runner's downturned palm. As the staggers unwind coming off the last bend the relative race positions of each team become apparent.

Teams from the United States have dominated the men's 4 × 100 metres event for most of this century, winning the sprint relay gold medals twelve times at the Olympic Games. In more recent years the East Germans have excelled in the women's event, capturing both the 1976 and 1980 Olympic sprint relay titles.

The world's leading men's national sprint relay teams would normally expect to clock inside 39.50 sec. for this event, whilst anything faster than 43.50 sec. for a women's national squad would also be of the highest world class. A team's overall time for a sprint relay will always be a couple of seconds faster than the individual team members' best 100 metres clockings combined because the runners on legs 2 to 4 have the benefit of a flying start.

4 × 400 metres relay: The initial $1\frac{1}{4}$ laps (500 m) of this four-lap race are run in lanes, the second-leg runners breaking for the inside lane at the beginning of the backstraight. This means that the teams remain in their separate lanes for the first changeover and the changeover zones in each lane are staggered, since there is still one more bend to run before the staggers completely unwind. As in the sprint relay, the changeover zones extend 10 m (33 ft) either side of the scratch line in each lane but no acceleration zones are required here because it is not essential in a race of this length that the changeovers should be executed at maximum speed. In fact, during the second and third changeovers, for which the zones in each lane are adjacent to one another, the outgoing runners assemble in a line on the edge of the changeover zones, 10 m behind the scratch line/finish line, and it would be foolhardy for anyone to start running before receiving the baton with the waiting runners so crowded together.

The first 200 m of each leg tends to be run very fast, as the leading runners try to establish a clear victory margin, whilst those trailing attempt to close any gaps which may have developed. A team's fortunes can change dramatically from lap to lap since some athletes may overreach themselves having started too fast, allowing stronger runners to pass their flagging rivals in the homestraight.

Split times are generally recorded for each 400 m leg as the baton, rather than the athlete, crosses the finish line. The runners on legs 2 to 4 invariably clock faster relay splits than their best individual 400 m times. This is due, in part, to the flying start advantage and to the psychological advantage of being able to draw on other competitors sharing the inside lane.

United States teams have long dominated men's 4 × 400 metres relay running, boasting ten Olympic titles in all. Equally dominant in the women's section are the East Germans, who set several world records and won every major international championship title open to them in this event during the 1970s; and they continue to reign supreme.

Any national men's team clocking faster than 3 min. 05.00 sec. for the 4 × 400 metres relay is of the highest world class, whilst a comparable performance for a national women's team would be anything faster than 3:30.00.

Receiving the baton quickly and getting away from the mêlée of incoming and outgoing runners is most important in the 4 × 400 metres relay.

US National 4 × 100 m Men's Team (L to R): Calvin Smith, Emmit King, Willie Gault and Carl Lewis

GDR National 4 × 100 m Women's Team: In winning the sprint relay final at the 1983 World Championships the GDR national women's squad of Silke Gladisch, Marita Koch, Ingrid Auerswald and Marlies Gohr completed their nation's hattrick of world, Olympic and European titles in this event. That same World Championships squad had earlier in the year set a world record of 41.53, which marked the GDR's ninth consecutive improvement of the record since 1973.

UK National 4 × 100 m

Women's Team: In recent years UK national women's sprint relay squads have figured among the best in the world. At the 1983 World Championships the UK team of Joan Baptiste, Kathy Cook, Bev Callender and Shirley Thomas finished runners-up to the GDR squad, duplicating their placing of the previous year at the 1982 European Championships. In filling the bronze medal position at the 1980 Moscow Olympics the UK team also set a superb Commonwealth record of 42.43, which remained unbeaten at the end of 1983.

US National 4 × 100 m Men's Team: In 1983 the American squad of Emmit King, Willie Gault, Calvin Smith and Carl Lewis smashed the sprint relay world record with a time of 37.86 to take the gold medals at the World Championships, and capture a world title that the USA is not likely to relinquish for many years. A US national team also holds the Olympic record at 38.19, set in Munich in 1972 and, in fact, the Americans have only ever lost one Olympic final, to Germany in 1960, in the history of the Olympic Games.

GDR National 4 × 400 m Women's Team: Women's teams from the GDR have dominated this event in recent years, running 8 of the 10 fastest times ever recorded up to the end of 1983. At the 1982 European Championships the GDR squad of Kirsten Siemon, Sabine Busch, Dagmar Rubsam and Marita Koch beat their nation's own 6-year-old world record with 3:19.04. The GDR women also won the World Championships race clocking 3:19.73, but three years earlier had been narrowly beaten at the Moscow Olympics by the Russians.

US National 4 × 400 m Men's Team: At the 1968 Mexico Olympics the American squad of Vince Matthews, Larry James, Ron Freeman and Lee Evans created a world record of 2:56.16 in winning their event, which rates as one of the greatest athletics performances ever. In all, US National teams have run the event in under 3 minutes on six occasions. Of the rest of the world's nations only national teams from Kenya have beaten that time, on two occasions. The Americans last lost an Olympic 4 × 400 metres relay final, to Jamaica, in 1952.

UK National 4 × 400 m Men's Team: One of the top European nations in this event for many years, the UK still has possession of the European record for this event of 3:00.46, set by the national team that took the silver medals at the 1972 Munich Olympics. The UK team for the 1982 European Championships finished a close second to the strong West German squad, whilst at the World Championships the following year the team of Ainsley Bennett, Gary Cook, Todd Bennett and Phil Brown took the bronze.

THE HURDLES

100/110 metres hurdles

All hurdles events are basically sprints over obstacles and all are run in lanes, the competitors adopting the standard crouch start off starting blocks. The 100 metres hurdles is purely a female preserve, whilst the 110 metres hurdles is exclusively a men's event, yet there are many similarities between the two. For example, ten hurdles have to be negotiated by each athlete in both events.

The 100 metres hurdles shares the same start line as the flat 100 metres sprint but the 110 metres hurdles starts from a scratch line situated exactly 10 m (approx. 33 ft) behind that for the women's event. The obstacles for all hurdles races are of the same frame-like design, constructed of metal with wooden tops, and must conform to strict internationally accepted specifications. The height of each hurdle has to be adjustable to suit the requirements of the particular race in which it is used. For the women's 100 metres hurdles the obstacles must be 0.84 m (2 ft 9 in) in height; the obstacles in the men's 110 metres hurdles are 1.07 m (3 ft 6 in). In any hurdles event the athlete's stature is obviously a factor, for the taller the individual the easier the hurdling action over the obstacles, assuming that the hurdler's leg length is propor-

tionately long. Therefore, the typical hurdler is, on average, somewhat taller than the typical sprinter.

The hurdles are positioned at intervals along the track in level rows so that each competitor has a set of ten obstacles in his lane. The hurdles are not fixed to the ground but are counterweighted at the base, so that a force of at least 3.6 kg (7.9 lb) is required to overturn them. The exact positioning of the hurdles in a particular event, in relation to the start and finish lines and to each other, is determined by standard international regulations; these positions are marked on the track to assist accurate placement of the obstacles. In the 100 metres hurdles the first obstacle is 13.0 m (43 ft) from the start line and the tenth 10.5 m (34 ft) from the finish, whilst a gap of 8.5 m (28 ft) separates each obstacle from its nearest neighbours. The corresponding distances for the 110 metres hurdles are 13.72 m, 14.02 m, and 9.14 m (45, 46 and 30 ft).

Good flat speed is, of course, important to the sprint hurdler but the most vital skill is an efficient hurdling technique. The experienced hurdler clears each obstacle quickly and smoothly, losing contact with the ground for as short a time as possible, since speed cannot be generated while the athlete is airborne. The hurdler always takes off from the same leg, flicking the other leg (leading leg) forwards over the obstacle and down on to the track again as quickly as possible, whilst

Phases of sprint hurdling: The leading hurdler, on the right, has almost regained contact with the track, pulling her trailing leg through to recommence the sprinting action, whilst those behind stretch for the barriers, barely skimming the hurdle tops with their leading legs.

the thigh of the take-off leg is swung up and carried horizontally over the hurdle, just skimming the top of it, before following through to recommence the sprinting action between the obstacles. To achieve this movement at all requires extensive hip mobility. Sprinting between the obstacles is no haphazard affair either, for the hurdler has to gauge his stride length to be able to take off from the same leg at exactly the same distance from each obstacle. The hurdler thus needs to develop a particular stride pattern, through training, which will be used in every race. This stride pattern involves an exact number of strides between the hurdles (normally 3 strides in sprint hurdles events) and from the start to the first hurdle, thereby ensuring a smooth transition from sprinting to hurdling and avoiding any hesitation which would lose valuable time.

Very often during a race various competitors will be seen to knock down perhaps several hurdles in their own lanes. The athletes are not penalised for this since they can only lose momentum, rather than gaining any advantage, by failing to clear hurdles cleanly. The competitors are not, however, permitted to trail a foot or leg around the side of an obstacle, rather than over the top of it. Any athlete doing this deliberately would be disqualified. In a sprint hurdles race it is only possible to trail an obstacle on the inside and outside lanes, as those in adjacent lanes are all touching. Close finishes are inevitable in these short sprint hurdles events and, as in flat sprints, the competitors employ a dip finish.

So precise is the hurdling technique of international-class hurdlers that the 10 obstacles increase the overall race time by no more than 1.5–2.5 seconds. Top international male sprint hurdlers regularly clock times of inside 13.80 sec. for the 110 metres hurdles, whilst anything faster than 14.40 is of good UK national standard. The corresponding times for the women's 100 metres hurdles would be 13.00 sec. and 13.50 sec., respectively.

The women's sprint hurdles event is another Eastern bloc stronghold, whereas the men's sprint hurdles (or high hurdles as the event is often termed) has long been dominated by athletes from the United States, who have won the 110 metres hurdles gold medal at all bar four Olympic Games. As in the men's sprints, black American high hurdlers tend to

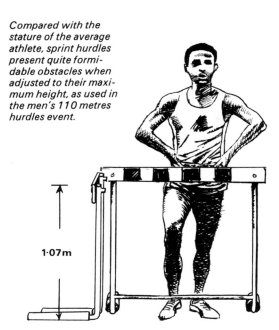

Compared with the stature of the average athlete, sprint hurdles present quite formidable obstacles when adjusted to their maximum height, as used in the men's 110 metres hurdles event.

1·07m

figure more prominently at top international level than their white counterparts.

400 metres hurdles

Often described as 'the mankiller' (female participation in this event did not gain official recognition until 1974), the 400 metres hurdles is both technically and physically demanding. The one-lap hurdler has to be able to maintain stride length and faultless hurdling technique right through to the tape, despite the inevitable fatigue experienced during the final stages of the race. Several years of extensive training and conditioning are required to equip an athlete with the necessary combination of strength, stamina and hurdling skill to excel at the highest level in this event.

The entire race is run in lanes and the staggered start is identical to that used in the flat 400 metres. Each competitor has to negotiate obstacles, as in the short sprint hurdles events, but because of the much greater length of the race the hurdles are lower, being only 0.914 m (3 ft) for the men and 0.762 m (2 ft 6 in) in the women's event. In both the men's and women's races the hurdles are placed in exactly the same location on the track; the first hurdle is situated 45 m (148 ft) from the scratch line in each lane; the ten obstacles are each spaced 35 m (115 ft) apart; and the last one is 40 m (131 ft) from the finish line.

From the spectator's point of view the 400 metres hurdles is an easier event to follow than the flat race, despite the staggers involved, for the hurdles are the same distances away from the scratch line in each lane and, therefore, the first athlete to rise at each flight of hurdles is the leader. As in all other hurdles races athletes are not penalized for knocking obstacles over in the 400 metres event. The problem here is that, as a result of the stagger, none of the hurdles is immediately adjacent to the other in the first 300 m, so the competitors must be careful not to risk disqualification through trailing a foot around the end of a hurdle.

Leg speed between the obstacles in the one-lap event is not quite as critical as for the pure sprint-hurdler but the stride pattern is just as important. International-class male 400 metres hurdlers usually take 13 strides between the hurdles in the early stages of a race, before fatigue sets in causing the stride length to shorten. The athlete is then forced to increase the number of strides between hurdles and in order to continue leading with the same leg he usually adds two more strides, running 15s the rest of the way. One or two very exceptional athletes are able to maintain 13 strides between hurdles for the full race distance. Top female internationals may begin a race with anything from 15 to 17 strides between hurdles, either maintaining that stride pattern throughout or increasing the number of strides in the second half of the race, as do the men. Even at international level athletes can be seen to misjudge their stride pattern through sheer fatigue towards the end of a race and, occasionally, a sure winner may throw the race away by stuttering or stumbling at the last hurdle.

Top male international 400 metres hurdlers are capable of

The danger of trailing a leg around the hurdles on a bend is far greater for an athlete using a right leg lead, as is the figure in the centre.

regularly bettering 50.00 sec. for their event, whilst male hurdlers of the highest UK national standard invariably clock times of faster than 51.50 sec. The corresponding performances for women of top international and UK national class would be sub 56.00 sec. and sub 59.00 sec., respectively, although rapid improvement in standards is expected in the next few years in this relatively new women's event.

Good 400 metres flat speed is the most basic essential for successful one-lap hurdling and, on average, top competitors run the 400 metres hurdles no more than 3–4 seconds slower than they would on the flat. In fact, several of the greatest ever 400 metres hurdlers have also excelled as 4×400 metres relay runners.

Thomas Munkelt (GDR)

Foster, Greg (USA): Born 14.8.1958. Only his great countryman Renaldo Nehemiah had ever run faster than his 1981 best of 13.03 for 110 metres hurdles up to the end of 1983. His first big win came in the 1981 World Cup but two years later he reached the pinnacle in his event taking the 110 metres hurdles gold medal in a time of 13.42 at the World Championships. In 1979 he figured in a unique indoor world best dead heat with Nehemiah, clocking 6.95 for 60 yards hurdles.

Holtom, Mark (UK): Born 6.2.1958. On the brink of top world class for several seasons, he finally made the breakthrough in 1982, smashing the UK 110 metres hurdles record three times,

finishing with 13.43 to take the silver medal at the Brisbane Commonwealth Games. Earlier successes include a 1977 European Junior Championships second place and a win in the 1981 European Cup final. Injury early in 1983 ruined an outside medal chance at the inaugural World Championships.

Jahn, Bettine (GDR): Born 3.8.1958. The latest in a long line of world-beating East German sprint hurdlers, she excelled at the 1983 World Championships winning the 100 metres hurdles gold medal in a wind-assisted 12.35, faster than the world record. Amazingly, this was her first major success, although she had missed the bronze medal at the 1982 European Championships by only 0.01 sec. and finished 7th in the 1980 Olympic final.

Kalek, Lucyna (Poland): Born 9.1.1956. Of her country's numerous female sprint hurdles stars over the years, she has one of the finest competitive records. Reaching world class in 1979 with a 100 metres hurdles victory at the World Student Games in a fast 12.62, she went on to take the sprint hurdles bronze medal at the 1980

Bettine Jahn (GDR)

Olympic Games. Two years later she crowned her career with a resounding 100 metres hurdles win at the European Championships in one of the fastest recorded times of 12.45.

Munkelt, Thomas (GDR): Born 3.8.1952. Europe's leading 110 metres hurdler for several years he has compiled an enviable competitive record without ever seriously challenging Frenchman Guy Drut's 1975 European sprint hurdles record of 13.28. In addition to several European indoor hurdles titles, three European Cup final wins (1977/79/83) and a World Cup victory in 1977, his greatest successes include European Championships hurdles titles in 1978 and 1982, in between which he became Olympic champion, though in the absence of the all-powerful Americans. Below top form in 1983 he could place only fifth at the World Championships.

Strong, Shirley (UK): Born 18.11.1958. The most talented British female sprint hurdler for many years, she finally broke into real world class in 1983. That year she three times broke the UK 100 metres hurdles record, clocking a season's best of 12.87 and placed fifth in the World Championships women's sprint hurdles final, having never previously reached an Olympic or European final. Her earlier career highlights include a second and first in the Commonwealth Games 100 metres hurdles finals of 1978 and 1982, respectively.

Ambrozene, Anna (USSR): Born 14.4.1955. A World Student Games win in the 400 metres hurdles in 1981 marked her out as an outstanding prospect but bad tactics deprived her of a medal at the 1982 European Championships. However, she set a world record of 54.02 early in 1983 and narrowly failed to take first place in her specialist event at that year's World Championships. She also placed second in the 1983 European Cup final race.

Morley, Sue (UK): Born 6.1.1960. She just missed out on a medal in the women's 400 metres hurdles at the 1982 Commonwealth Games but began to realize her obvious potential in 1983. Breaking 57 seconds for the first time early that year, she reached the World Championships final finishing 7th with a UK record of 56.04. Shortly after that she achieved an excellent third place in the women's European Cup final 400 metres hurdles behind two World Championships medallists.

Moses, Edwin (USA): Born 31.7.1955. Throughout the history of athletics few athletes have dominated an event as totally as this man

Edwin Moses (USA)

has. Since winning the 1976 Olympic Games 400 metres hurdles final in world record time (47.64), he has won every major international race that he has contested, including the 1977, 1979 and 1981 World Cup races and the inaugural World Championships final in 1983. In fact, he had won more than 90 straight races during the six years up to the end of 1983 and had clocked the nine fastest ever 400 metres hurdles during that period. He recorded his fourth world record, of 47.02, in 1983.

Oakes, Gary (UK): Born 21.9.1958. One of the smallest international 400 metres hurdlers at 1.77 m (5 ft 9¾ in), he excelled in placing third in the 1980 Olympic final clocking a lifetime best of 49.11, the fourth fastest time by a Briton. Back in 1977, he had taken the 400 metres hurdles bronze medal at the European Junior Championships but has yet to again approach his Moscow Olympics form.

Schmid, Harald (FRG): Born 29.9.1957. The greatest ever European 400 metres hurdler, he was the first man to retain a European title at this event, winning in 1978 and 1982. His European record of 47.48, set in 1982, made him the second fastest 400 metres hurdler ever, behind Ed Moses, and in 1983 he took second place behind the American in the World Championships race. As well as European Cup final hurdles wins in 1979 and 1983 he also won the flat 400 metres in the earlier year and has figured in several West German 4 × 400 metres relay squads, earning European gold (1978 and 1982), World Championships silver (1983) and Olympic bronze (1976) medals.

Anna Ambrozene (USSR)

Skoglund, Anne-Louise (Sweden): Born 28.6.1962. A former world junior record holder for 400 metres hurdles (56.68 in 1980), she proved herself to be the top European in her event in 1982, clocking 54.58 to take the European Championships 400 metres hurdles gold medal, while still only 20. Despite running 54.80 in the 1983 World Championships race at Helsinki, she placed only sixth, but must have her best performances still to come within the next few years.

3000 METRES STEEPLECHASE

The steeplechase is unlike any other race on the track in that the race distance would qualify it as a middle distance event, yet the obstacles which have to be negotiated make it as demanding as a long distance race. Even the women, who now participate in many events which were once exclusively male preserves, have not dared to make a serious assault on this most gruelling of endurance events.

The obstacles used are of two types but the majority are movable barriers which are intended to stand firm when struck, being constructed of solid timber and weighing up to 100 kg (220 lb). These barriers are 0.91 m (3 ft) high and extend across the three inside lanes of the track. A permanently sited obstacle, known as the water jump, is situated just inside the track kerb on the top bend. It consists of a fixed barrier, similar to the other barriers, and a 3.66 m (12 ft) square expanse of water behind the barrier with a maximum depth of 70 cm (27½ in) at the barrier end. At some stadia the water jump is located just outside the main track.

Where the water jump is situated inside the track kerb, the

Although the steeple-chaser clears the movable barriers (see inset diagram) as would a sprint hurdler, the overall length of the water jump obstacle makes it impossible to hurdle. Here, the runner must push off hard from the top of the barrier in order to land in the shallower far end of the water-filled pit.

track has to be shortened (usually to 390 m), by removing two sections of the kerb either side of the top bend, to take in the obstacle. To ensure that the race distance is exactly 3000 metres, where the track will be shortened to 390 m, the start line has to be 270 m from the finish, approximately halfway along the backstraight. The runners do not have to clear any obstacles during the initial 270 m of the race but as they approach the finishing post for the first time, the barriers are placed on the track and the top bend kerb adjusted so that four barriers and one water jump are negotiated during each of the seven full laps (a total of 35 barriers in all). The five obstacles are spaced exactly 78 m (256 ft) apart around the track, the first barrier on each lap being situated at least 10 m (33 ft) after the finish line. As in the longer flat races, lap indicator boards are used and times are announced for each lap (normally 390 m) and/or kilometre.

Spectators will see that barriers are negotiated by virtually any method, such as jumping over, vaulting, or even stepping on the barrier but the experienced steeplechaser conserves energy by cleanly hurdling the obstacles, as would a sprint hurdler, although he must not trail a leg around the side of an obstacle. In contrast, the water jump cannot be effectively

cleared without putting a foot on the barrier and the runners must go through or over the water, rather than around it.

Steeplechasing tactics are similar to those of the long distance events, although the problem of lapped runners rarely arises in races of international class at this relatively short distance. The steeplechaser's primary concern is to maintain an economic running rhythm and conserve energy, as far as the effort of continually negotiating obstacles will allow. The effects of rapidly increasing fatigue during the latter stages of a race become obvious as athletes' hurdling form over the barriers deteriorates and runners drag leaden legs out of the water jump. The race is never truly decided until the last barrier has been successfully cleared, for even race favourites have come to grief at the final water jump or barrier. Fast last laps in this event are a rarity, with only a handful of athletes ever having clocked under 60 sec. for the final circuit.

Times of anything faster than 8 min. 25.0 sec. would be of the highest international class, whereas under 8:35.0 would be of top national standard among UK steeplechasers.

Ilg, Patriz (FRG): Born 5.12.1957. He started his athletics career as a flat runner, gaining second place over 3000 metres at the 1975 European Junior Championships, but eventually turned to the steeplechase where he quickly excelled, taking the silver medal at the 1978 European Championships. Following injury and a period of indifferent form he came back in 1982 to win the European Steeplechase title, and the very next year became world champion in his chosen event with his best time of 8:15.06. His hallmark is a blistering sprint finish.

Patriz Ilg (FRG)

Marsh, Henry (USA): Born 15.3.1954. The unluckiest athlete in his event, he finished first in the 1981 World Cup steeplechase but was disqualified for running around a barrier and in 1983, at the World Championships, he looked certain for the silver medal before falling over the final barrier. However, he won the 1979 Pan-American Games and ran the fastest times in the world in both 1982 (8:16.17) and 1983 (8:12.37).

Reitz, Colin (UK): Born 5.4.1960. One of the most competitive British steeplechasers for years, he also brings exceptional miling speed (3:55.41 in 1982) to this event. He was European junior 2 km steeplechase silver medallist in 1979 but made the greatest progress in 1982, setting a UK 3000 metres steeplechase record of 8:18.80. He excelled in the 1983 World Championships steeplechase taking the bronze medal with another UK record (8:17.75) and later the same month took second place in the European Cup final race.

POLE VAULT

The most spectacular of field events, the pole vault, which is contested only by men, requires the athlete to catapult himself as high as possible above the ground and over a crossbar using a fibreglass pole and relying on his own strength and speed to supply the necessary propulsion.

The hollow metal crossbar which the vaulter has to lever himself over is suspended between two height-adjustable supports attached to a pair of tall metal stands (or uprights) placed at least 3.66 m (12 ft) apart. The crossbar can only be dislodged in the direction of the landing area, which is situated behind the uprights and resembles a large square mattress, usually containing foam rubber and at least 1 m (3 ft) in height: thick enough to break the vaulter's fall and prevent his injury. Sunk into the runway, immediately beneath the uprights, is a 20 cm (8 in) deep sloping metal box in which the vaulter places (or 'plants') the end of the pole before take-off. Surprisingly, the average 5 m (16 ft) long fibreglass pole weighs as little as 2 kg (4½ lb) and can be bent to an angle of 90°. These poles vary in their degree of flexibility to suit vaulters of different bodyweights and strength. The end of the pole held by the vaulter is bound with sticky tape and to improve the grip still further athletes will be seen to apply adhesive resin to their hands before each vault.

The run up is all-important and has to be judged carefully. To begin vaulting the athlete holds the pole horizontally and sprints down the runway, generating as much speed and momentum as possible before take-off. A split-second prior to take-off the far end of the pole is lowered into the box, the athlete using his bodyweight to pull on and bend the pole. Simultaneously, he lifts his feet and hips vertically upwards, being carried feet first towards the bar as the pole straightens. Finally, the vaulter twists his body round, fleetingly performing a handstand on top of the pole before pushing away from it (so that it doesn't knock the bar off) and curling over the bar. Once airborne the vaulter must not reposition his hands or 'climb' the pole. The vaulter registers a failure if his pole or part of his body either knocks the bar off or touches the ground or landing area beyond the plane of the uprights before he clears the bar and also, if he does not take his vault

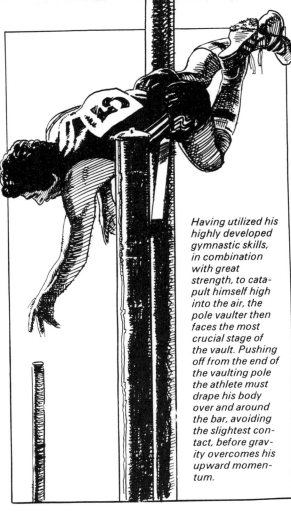

Having utilized his highly developed gymnastic skills, in combination with great strength, to catapult himself high into the air, the pole vaulter then faces the most crucial stage of the vault. Pushing off from the end of the vaulting pole the athlete must drape his body over and around the bar, avoiding the slightest contact, before gravity overcomes his upward momentum.

within a certain time limit. A successful vault still remains valid if, subsequently, the pole passes under the bar or strong winds blow it down. Cold, wet and windy weather adversely affects vaulting, so vaulters often use a range of poles of different flexibility to adapt to such conditions.

During a competition the bar is gradually raised (by perhaps 5–10 cm (2–4 in) at a time), after all the competitors have attempted the previous height. A vaulter may, however, enter the competition at any point above a specified starting height and can then elect to attempt any subsequent height. Each vaulter may make three attempts at any one height but once he has registered three consecutive failures at the same or different heights, he is out of the competition and is credited with his highest clearance. A vault is not counted as a failure if, as occasionally happens, the pole breaks in mid-vault. If a record vault is attempted the height of the bar has to be measured before and, if successful, after the vault.

If two or more vaulters clear the same height the athlete with the fewest attempts at that height is awarded the better placing. Failing that, the lowest number of failures during the competition is the deciding factor and after that the lowest number of jumps. The very last resort is a jump-off between the tying athletes, but only if the tie is for first place. It is, therefore, in the vaulter's interests to plan his competition so that he takes as few vaults as possible, registering the minimum of failures. A competition will usually continue until a winner is decided and at international level it is not unusual for a competition to last up to eight hours. Therefore, the vaulters need to conserve energy in order to produce their best vaulting in the latter stages of the event.

International-class vaulters normally aspire to heights greater than 5.60 m (18 ft 4½ in). United Kingdom pole vaulting standards have lagged behind those of the world's leading nations in this event since the early part of the century and today British vaulters scaling more than 5.00 m (16 ft 5 in) are among the country's best.

No other athletics event has been so totally dominated by one nation throughout its history as has the pole vault. The United States supplied the pole vault winner at every Olympic Games (16 in all) from 1896 to 1968 and virtually monopolized the event world record during that period.

Stock, Keith (UK): Born 18.3.1957. His pole vault victory in the 1981 European Cup semi-finals ranks as the most significant British achievement in this event since Geoff Elliott's 1954 European Championships bronze medal success. In addition, his 1981 Commonwealth and UK pole vault record of 5.65 m (18 ft 6½ in) represented the closest approach to the existing world record (within 16 cm) by any British vaulter this century.

Vigneron,   Thierry (France): Born 9.3.1960. The first man to pole vault 19 feet (5.80 m/19 ft 0¼ in), he is a prolific record breaker in this event yet has continually failed to perform well under major competition pressure. In 1979 he set a world junior pole vault record which still stood at the end of 1983; in 1980 he twice vaulted a world record 5.75 m (18 ft 10¼ in) but placed only 7th at the Olympics; in 1983 he placed only 8th at the World Championships and then set another record of 5.83 m (19 ft 1½ in).

Volkov,   Konstantin (USSR): Born 28.2.1960. The world's leading vaulter of 1981, he placed first in the World Student Games, European Cup and World Cup competitions and achieved a vault of 5.84 m (19 ft 2 in) at an unofficial meeting to exceed the then world record by 3 cm. His finest performances include silver medal winning vaults at both the 1980 Olympic Games and 1983 World Championships and he has remained a tremendously consistent vaulter over several seasons in one of athletics' most difficult events.

Konstantin Volkov (USSR)

HIGH JUMP

In the high jump—a contest of pure vertical jumping ability—
a competitor's success or failure is, more often than not,
immediately apparent: the crossbar either remains precari-
ously in place or is knocked down.

The high jump equipment consists of a pair of metal stands
placed at least 3.66 m (12 ft) apart, each with a height-
adjustable peg on which the crossbar rests so that it can fall
backwards when struck. Behind the stands is the square,
raised, foam rubber filled landing area on to which the jumpers
will fall, from heights perhaps in excess of 2.13 m (7 ft).

Height is a distinct advantage in this event and international
high jumpers of both sexes are invariably tall (statures greater
than 1.90 m (6 ft 3 in) for men and 1.76 m (5 ft 9 in) for
women are common). Yet jumpers ideally need to be lightly
built with sufficient leg strength and spring to be able to
propel their bodyweight to a height perhaps 20–30 cm (8–
12 in) over their own heads.

When jumping the athlete runs up to the bar, sometimes
from well outside the semicircular edge of the high jump fan,
converting momentum into vertical lift on take-off, from one
foot only, just in front of the bar, which is striped to assist
sighting. The run-up has to be very precise, and spectators
will see most jumpers placing markers on the runway to help
them judge the approach, so as to arrive at the exact take-off
point on the same take-off leg each jump. Even a fractional
approach error may result in a failed jump.

Two main jumping styles are currently in favour. The most
recent, the 'Fosbury flop' involves clearing the bar headfirst
and backwards, the athlete landing on the neck and shoulders.
With the more traditional 'straddle' style the jumper takes off
facing the bar, clearing it face downwards as the body rotates
lengthways around the bar. A jumper registers a failure if part
of his body knocks the bar off, touches the ground or landing
area beyond the plane of the uprights without first clearing
the bar or if the jump is not taken within a certain time limit. A
successful jump is not invalidated if the bar is subsequently
dislodged by strong winds. Poor weather conditions do not
affect high jumping quite as severely as pole vaulting, although
a wet run up surface can upset some athletes' approach run.

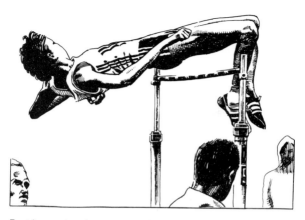

Fast becoming the most popular high jumping style, the 'Fosbury flop' requires the jumper to arch backwards over the bar, taking care not to clip it off with the heels.

In competition the high jump bar is raised by 3–5 cm (1–2 in) after each round but otherwise the rules for competition and for tie situations are basically the same as for the pole vault (see p. 120). A jumper will often stand motionless for up to a minute before jumping, concentrating intensely in order to blot out all distractions. He does this because a high jump competition is as much a psychological battle as a physical one with athletes endeavouring to clear each height first time or even bypassing a height altogether to pressure rivals into making mistakes.

The best international male jumpers regularly surpass 2.25 m (7 ft 4¾ in) while the top female jumpers clear upwards of 1.90 m (6 ft 3 in). High jumping standards in the UK are relatively poor with only the very best male and female jumpers clearing heights in excess of 2.15 m (7 ft 0¾ in) and 1.83 m (6 ft), respectively.

Today, much of the world's high jumping talent is concentrated in Europe and the USA, with but a few outstanding individuals emerging from the other continents.

Bykova, Tamara (USSR): Born 21.12.1958. Only the second Russian woman to set a high jump world record, when scaling 2.04 m (6 ft $8\frac{1}{4}$ in) in 1983, she opened a new era in the women's event. Runner-up positions in the high jump at both the 1981 World Cup and 1982 European Championships showed her potential but in 1983 she improved dramatically, surpassing the outdoor world record with 2.03 m (6 ft 8 in), at the European Indoor Championships, before becoming the first women's high jump world champion, in Helsinki. Although only runner-up at the 1983 European Cup final she still equalled the then world record of 2.03 m.

Jian-Hua, Zhu (China): Born 29.5.1963. When high jumping 2.37 m (7 ft $9\frac{1}{4}$ in) and 2.38 m (7 ft $9\frac{3}{4}$ in) in 1983 he became the first male athlete from the People's Republic of China to set official athletics world records. His major high jump victories prior to 1983 came at the 1981 Asian Championships and 1982 Asian Games where he cleared 2.33 m (7 ft $8\frac{3}{4}$ in), the second highest jump in the world that year. He gained his country's only medal at the 1983 World Championships taking the high jump bronze with a 2.29 m (7 ft 6 in) clearance.

Marti, Debbie (UK): Born Switzerland 14.5.1968. An exciting new British female high jumping talent, she jumped 1.88 m (6 ft 2 in) in 1983 at the age of 15 to exceed anything previously achieved by a British teenager. Competing against girls two and three years her senior at the European Junior Championships that year she performed brilliantly, filling the bronze medal position

Tamara Bykova (USSR)

with her second 1.88 m clearance of the season.

Meyfarth, Ulrike (FRG): Born 4.5.1956. Having become the youngest athletics Olympic champion in an individual event, when winning the high jump at the age of 16 in 1972, she had to wait 10 years before capturing her next major title at the 1982 European Championships. She set world records of 1.92 m (6 ft 3¾ in) and 2.02 m (6 ft 7½ in), respectively, in winning those titles and achieved a third record mark of 2.03 m (6 ft 8 in) in winning the 1983 European Cup final event. She finished runner-up to Tamara Bykova at the 1983 World Championships.

Mogenburg,   Dietmar (FRG): Born 15.8.1961. A precocious high jump talent in his youth he placed first in both the European Junior Championships and European Cup final when only 17, and the following year took the European indoor title and became world record holder jumping 2.35 m (7 ft 8½ in) while still only 18. His Olympic medal hopes were dashed by the West German boycott in 1980 but two years later he made amends, capturing the European high jump title with 2.30 m (7 ft 6½ in).

Parsons, Geoff (UK): Born 14.8.1964. Certainly the tallest (2.03 m/6 ft 8 in) and potentially one of the finest ever British high jumpers, he set a UK record of 2.25 m (7 ft 4½ in) in 1983 when only 18. The previous year he was already good enough to be the highest placed British jumper at the AAA Championships and earned selection for both the European Championships and Commonwealth Games, placing a commendable 7th in the high jump final at the latter event.

Dietmar Mogenburg (FRG)

TRIPLE JUMP

The most demanding of the jumping events, the triple jump (or hop, step and jump) requires such strength and resilience that it is confined to male competitors only. Consisting of three distinct phases this is also, technically, a very complex event. The top-class triple jumper requires a diverse range of abilities including speed, co-ordination and balance combined with tough, powerful legs which have to take a terrific pounding during a competition.

Initially, the jumper has to build up sprinting speed on the runway to produce the necessary momentum for the take-off. The athlete judges his run-up, aided by markers placed alongside the runway, so that he knows exactly how many strides will bring him just on to the white take-off board. He must then control and distribute his effort evenly over the three phases. Taking off on the hop phase, from either leg (1) (2) (3), the jumper swings the inactive (sleeping) leg backwards to maintain balance (4), whilst the take-off leg is swung forwards ready for the first landing (5). Leg strength is essential here, for the take-off leg has to absorb the body's impact on landing and instantaneously supply the drive for the take-off on the step phase (6). The jumper virtually hangs in the air (7) during the step phase, with the take-off leg

trailing, prior to landing on the opposite leg (8). After clearing almost two-thirds of the overall jumping distance during the first two phases the jumper then has to generate maximum lift for the jump phase (9) (10) (11), thrusting his legs forward at the last moment to gain extra distance on touchdown (12) in the sand-filled landing pit. International athletes may clear in excess of 6.00 m (19 ft 8 in) on the final jump phase alone. A valid jump will be measured from the front edge of the take-off board to the nearest mark in the sand made by any part of the jumper's body.

A number of factors can invalidate what may look a technically good jump. For example, the athlete can land on the 13 m (42 ft 6 in) long section of runway between the take-off board and the sandpit during the three phases but he must not overstep the take-off board during the initial take-off. If he does, his shoe will leave a mark on the no-jump indicator (a layer of Plasticine bordering the front edge of the 20 cm (8 in) wide take-off board), rendering his effort a foul or no-jump. After the initial take-off the jumper must complete the hop and step phases landing first on the same take-off leg and then on the opposite leg. Any other sequence invalidates the jump. Also, the inactive leg must not touch the ground before the final landing. Neither should a competitor walk back through the sandpit after jumping. Finally, the jumper must make his attempt within a $1\frac{1}{2}$ minute time limit.

Each competitor is allowed six jumps (including fouls) during a competition, except in a major championship when only the leading eight athletes may have three more jumps, following completion of the first three rounds of jumping. The relative length of each athlete's best jump determines his final placing in the competition. If there is a tie the athlete with the longest second jump is placed highest. In the unlikely event that a tie then still remains unresolved, third best jumps, and so on, are compared.

The experienced triple jumper will often begin a competition with a safe valid jump, rather than a long one, to avoid the possibility of his producing a series of fouls which would effectively eliminate him. After that, he would endeavour to improve on his first-round jump. Traditionally the fireworks begin in the final round when the competitors throw caution to the wind in an all-out effort to produce a last big jump which could win or place highly.

Cold, wet weather tends to reduce the triple jumper's efficiency, whereas competing with a following wind or in the thin atmosphere of high altitudes is a positive advantage to this and other explosive events such as the sprints and long jump.

Marks in excess of 16.75 m (54 ft $11\frac{1}{2}$ in) would be expected of top international jumpers. Triple jumping standards in the UK are better than they have ever been with the top jumpers reaching 16.00 m (52 ft 6 in) plus.

Before the turn of the century the earliest pioneers of the triple jump often employed a method of jumping which involved two hops and a jump, which usually produced superior results compared with the now traditional triple jumping style. In 1896 American James Connolly won the inaugural Olympic title using the two-hop style. The event was dominated by Irish and US athletes before World War I and by Japanese and Australian jumpers between the great wars. Since World War II, European nations have produced the majority of Olympic champions and world record holders, the strongest challenge to European supremacy coming from several exceptional Brazilian jumpers.

Banks, Willie (USA): Born 11.3.1956. A great character and crowd pleaser, he first came to prominence in 1979 winning the World Student Games triple jump title and placing second at the Pan-American Games. In 1981 he produced the longest ever legal jump at sea level of 17.56 m (57 ft $7\frac{1}{2}$ in) and early the following year jumped a world indoor best of 17.41 m (57 ft $1\frac{1}{2}$ in). He lead the triple jump competition for four rounds at the 1983 World Championships but eventually finished runner-up, jumping 17.18 m (56 ft $4\frac{1}{2}$ in).

Connor, Keith (UK): Born 16.9.1957. Easily the most outstanding British triple jumper ever, he was ranked No. 1 in the world in his event in 1982, winning both Commonwealth and European titles (the first Briton to win a European Championships triple jump medal) and registering the second longest legal jump ever recorded of 17.57 m (57 ft $8\frac{3}{4}$ in). He had also won the Commonwealth triple jump title at the 1978 Games and was the first Briton to exceed 17 metres (17.16 m (56 ft $3\frac{3}{4}$ in) in 1980) in the event. One of the favourites for the 1983

Keith Connor (UK)

World Championships triple jump, he surprisingly failed to qualify for the final.

Hoffman, Zdzislaw (Poland): Born 27.8.1959. The biggest shock of the 1983 World Championships was this man's victory in the triple jump final. Never having previously competed in a major international event, he produced a Polish national record jump of 17.42 m (57 ft 2 in) to beat the best in the world for the gold medal. Just two weeks later he was beaten into second place during the European Cup final competition.

LONG JUMP

Long jumping is one of the simplest and most natural of athletic activities and, as in the sprints, natural ability plays a large part in an athlete's success at this event. The top-class long jumper is invariably strongly built, with good sprinting speed and explosive jumping power. The fact that female long jumpers have a lower strength to bodyweight ratio than men is reflected in their comparatively shorter jumping distances. At international level women's performances on average fall short of the men's by some 1.25 m (4 ft 1 in) or more.

As in the triple jump an accurately paced run-up is all-important to the long jumper, who must step just on to the take-off board without having to chop stride and lose vital speed. The standard 45 m (147 ft) runway will allow top jumpers around 19 to 21 strides to reach the take-off board. On take-off, from either leg, the jumper must gain as much height as possible so that momentum can have the optimum effect, carrying the athlete the greatest possible distance through the air. Once airborne the athlete will employ one of two jumping styles, known as the 'hitchkick' and the 'hang', to counteract the rotational movement imparted to the body at take-off. Nothing that the athlete does in the air can materially increase the distance jumped but these jumping styles prevent the unnecessary loss of jumping distance through poor jumping technique. With the 'hitchkick' the jumper appears to take one or two strides in mid-air, before drawing the legs forward for landing. In the 'hang' technique the athlete's body seemingly hangs in the air prior to the arms and legs being thrust forward for landing. Throwing the arms forward tends to prevent the athlete from falling backwards on impact and shortening the jump. The jump is measured in exactly the same way as for the triple jump.

The rules governing what constitutes a no-jump are similar to those applying to the triple jump, except that the long jumper may not touch the 1.0 m (3 ft) long section of runway between the take-off board and the sandpit. Similarly, rules relating to the number of jumps each individual is allowed during a competition, and to the way in which a tie is resolved, are identical for both of the horizontal jumps.

Left: *The running motion typical of the 'hitchkick' technique.*
Right: *The 'hang' jumper appears as if suspended in mid-air.*

Windy conditions can make it difficult for horizontal jumpers to judge their run-up accurately, but in general long jumpers tend to register fewer no-jumps in competition than do triple jumpers, probably because the long jump is technically less complex. However, the experienced long jumper still likes to get in a solid but safe opening jump early in the competition, saving the biggest effort for the latter stages.

Top international male long jumpers need to be capable of marks in excess of 8.00 m (26 ft 3 in), whilst their female counterparts, the majority of whom represent the Eastern bloc countries, would expect to better 6.70 m (22 ft). Long jumpers from the UK registering marks of better than 7.60 m (24 ft 11 in) (men) and 6.30 m (20 ft 8 in) (women) would be considered in the top bracket.

The long jump is another of the events requiring explosive sprinting speed and which has long been dominated by male athletes from the United States. American athletes have won the men's Olympic long jump title on all but three occasions since 1896. Two of the most outstanding individual athletics performances in the history of the sport were set in this event by American men, namely marks of 8.13 m (26 ft 8¼ in) by the great Jesse Owens in 1936, and a phenomenal 8.90 m (29 ft 2½ in) by Bob Beamon at the 1968 Mexico Olympic Games.

Cusmir, Anisoara (Romania): Born 28.6.1962. Not even a 6 metre long jumper until 1980, she achieved the astonishing distance of 7.43 m (24 ft 4½ in) in 1983, to add 22 cm to the previous world record, for the biggest single improvement in the history of the women's event. She placed second at both the 1981 World Student Games and 1982 European Championships and despite her superb form in 1983, again finished runner-up in the long jump at the World Championships, reaching a very creditable 7.15 m (23 ft 5½ in).

Anisoara Cusmir (Romania)

Daute, Heike (GDR): Born 16.12.1964. Perhaps the most outstanding talent ever in women's long jump, she first exceeded 7 metres in 1981, when only 16, in winning the European junior girls long jump title by a staggering 59 cm margin. She missed out on a medal at the 1982 European Championships but confirmed her earlier promise the very next year, becoming the women's world long jump champion in Helsinki with a wind-assisted leap of 7.27 m (23 ft 10¼ in), second only to the world record.

Dombrowski, Lutz (GDR): Born 25.6.1959. In winning the 1980 Olympic long jump title, he became the first man to exceed 28 feet (actually 8.54 m/28 ft 0¼ in) at sea level. Although he always preferred the triple jump, he achieved the highest world class as a long jumper by the time he was 20, winning his event in the European Cup final and placing second at the World Cup during 1979. After a lay off in 1981 he came back to take the 1982 European title with another big winning jump of 8.41 m (27 ft 7¼ in).

Kinch, Bev (UK): Born 14.1.1964. The British girl most likely to challenge the best in the world at women's long jump in the next few years, she finally beat Mary Rand's 19-year-old UK record when jumping 6.90 m (22 ft 7¾ in) for fifth place at the 1983 World Championships. She gave an indication of things to come in 1982, taking the long jump bronze medal at the Commonwealth Games and in 1983, just prior to the World Championships, displayed phenomenal speed, winning the 1983 World Student Games 100 metres title in 11.13 w.

Lewis, Carl (USA): Born 1.7.1961. Unquestionably the greatest long jumper that ever lived, his 1983 best of 8.79 m (28 ft 10¼ in) must be intrinsically superior to Bob Beamon's 1968 altitude-assisted world record of 8.90 m (29 ft 2½ in). A Pan-American Games long jump bronze medallist in 1979, he gained his first big win in the World Cup competition of 1981. He underlined his superiority at the first World Championships taking only two jumps in the competition, to achieve a 26 cm victory margin with his winner of 8.55 m (28 ft 0¾ in).

Carl Lewis (USA)

Thompson, Daley (UK): Born 3.7.1958. As the greatest all-rounder that ever lived (see Multi-events: Personalities) he is particularly outstanding in the long jump, being one of only three Britons to have leapt 8.00 m (26 ft 3 in) or more without wind assistance. His windy long jump of 8.11 m (26 ft 7¼ in) during the 1978 Commonwealth Games decathlon competition would also have won the individual event, while in 1982 and 1983 his best marks were good enough to top the UK men's long jump rankings.

133

HAMMER THROW

Of the four throwing events in track and field athletics the hammer—restricted to male competitors only—is undoubtedly the most dramatic to watch and probably the most dangerous. Like all throwers of international standard the top-class hammer specialist tends to be big and powerful, averaging 100 kg (220 lb) plus bodyweight, yet he still needs to be quick on his feet and possess perfect balance.

The hammer itself consists of a solid metal ball connected to a metal handle by a length of spring steel wire. The total weight of the implement is 7.260 kg (16 lb) for an overall length of 121.5 cm (3 ft 11¾ in). The athlete throws the hammer from a flat concrete circle measuring 2.13 m (7 ft) in diameter and because there is always the danger that the implement might be accidentally released in some direction other than towards the landing area (sector), the sides and rear of the throwing area are surrounded by a protective cage constructed of steel uprights from which a heavy gauge hemp net is suspended. The thrower releases the hammer in the direction of the infield, endeavouring to keep it inside the lines bordering the 40° landing sector.

Facing away from the landing sector at the rear of the circle,

On the final turn the thrower will be seen to pull down on the hammer handle to impart maximum velocity to the hammer head.

the thrower holds the hammer handle with both hands and begins the throw by swinging the implement in a wide arc for a couple of revolutions (winding-up) while his trunk remains stationary. Then, holding the hammer at arm's length, the athlete spins around, building up the speed of the hammer head with every turn. The thrower will be seen to perform three or four complete revolutions in total and on the last turn he pulls hard on the hammer before lifting it powerfully upwards, using his back and leg muscles, prior to releasing the implement. Such is the friction created as the hammer handle leaves the thrower's hands that he must wear a glove for protection.

The sector is marked out with a number of arc lines at 10 m (33 ft) intervals to enable spectators to gauge the length of a throw (the exact distance of existing world and national records may also be indicated) but, often, the thrower's reaction as the implement lands will reveal whether the throw was good or bad. The actual distance thrown will be displayed on a manual or electronic scoreboard, usually situated behind the throwing area during all throwing events. The measurement is taken from the inside edge of the throwing circle to the nearest mark made by the implement in the landing sector.

If the athlete loses his rhythm before completing the throw

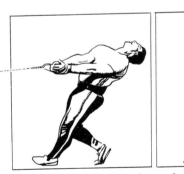

Co-ordinating leg and back muscles to produce a powerful lifting action, the thrower sends the hammer high into the air.

he may start again only if the hammer head has not touched the ground outside the circle during the trial. A throw is not valid if: the hammer lands outside the 40° sector; the thrower touches the ground outside the circle when throwing; the thrower leaves the circle before the hammer has landed or he does not leave the circle from the rear half; or if the thrower does not take his throw within the 1½ minute time limit. If the hammer breaks during a throw another trial is allowed.

Each competitor may have six throws unless, as in the case of a major championship, only the leading eight throwers, after three rounds, go on to take three more trials. Final placings are decided on the relative lengths of each competitor's best throw and a tie between two or more athletes is decided in the same way as for the horizontal jumping events.

Because of its greater complexity, there is probably more likelihood of no-throws in the hammer compared to other throwing events. However, the confident athlete may go for the big throw straight away to pressure his rivals, while others may play it safe with a valid throw before improving on their throwing distances and overall competition placings.

Nowadays, a thrower has to be capable of 75.00 m (246 ft 1 in) to be considered of top international class. The Russians are currently the undisputed world leaders in the hammer, having supplied all three medallists at both the 1980 Olympic Games and 1982 European Championships. In general, UK standards are not particularly high in this event with only a few throwers capable of exceeding 65.00 m (213 ft 3 in). In fact, throughout modern Olympic and European Championships history, only one bronze medal apiece has fallen to British athletes in this event.

The hammer cage serves as an essential safety measure during hammer throwing.

Sergey Litvinov (USSR)

Litvinov, Sergey (USSR): Born 23.1.1958. One of the smallest of world class hammer throwers, he is able to generate phenomenal speed in the throwing circle which, allied to his faultless throwing technique, has brought him several world records in this event. His best throw to the end of 1983 measured 84.14 m (276 ft 0 in). Having gained the reputation of cracking under pressure in big competitions (he placed second at the 1980 Olympic Games and only third at the 1982 European Championships) he finally came good in Helsinki in 1983, collecting the hammer gold medal at the World Championships with a big first round throw of 82.68 m (271 ft 3 in).

Sedykh, Yuriy (USSR): Born 11.6.1955. In contrast to countryman Sergey Litvinov he has always produced his best in major competition. Starting with the European junior hammer title in 1973, he became Olympic champion in 1976 and retained that title four years later in Moscow. He also won European Championships gold medals in both 1978 and 1982. The bubble finally burst at the World Championships in 1983 where he filled the runner-up spot behind Litvinov. He set three world hammer throwing records in 1980, the longest measuring 81.80 m (268 ft 4 in).

Weir, Robert (UK): Born 4.2.1961. Having trained in the USA for several years while at university there, he achieved his first major success at the 1982 Commonwealth Games, taking the gold medal with a new UK hammer record of 75.08 m (246 ft 4 in) (the first 75 metres plus throw by a Briton). He is also a top international-class discus thrower and placed a very respectable fifth in that event at the European Cup finals of 1981 and 1983.

SHOT PUT

The biggest and most powerful individuals in the sport of athletics are to be seen in this event. Male shot putters of international standard invariably weigh upwards of 115 kg (253 lb) for an average height of 1.90 m (6 ft 3 in), while the best females will generally top 85 kg (187 lb) and be 1.75 m (5 ft 9 in) tall.

The cannonball-like shot used by the men in this event is a 7.260 kg (16 lb) implement, whilst the women wield a smaller 4 kg (8.8 lb) version. The shot is put from a circle identical to that used for the hammer event, except that a 10 cm (4 in) high curved wooden stopboard is located at the front of the circle and the circle's concrete surface is lightly stippled so that the athlete will not slip on it. No protective cage is required as the thrower has complete control over the implement prior to release. The shot must land within the 40° sector which is marked out, as in the hammer event, enabling the spectators to judge more accurately the distances achieved.

The athlete using the popular 'O'Brien' putting style begins his effort from the back of the circle, facing away from the landing sector, with the shot held in one hand close to the neck. The athlete then moves backwards across the circle until his foot touches the side of the stopboard, from which point he pivots on his foremost leg, turning his body towards the front of the circle (glide phase). Finally, he pushes the shot out to arm's length with as much speed and elevation as possible, bracing his foot against the stopboard to help him stay in the circle. At no point should the shot be taken behind the line of the shoulders as if in a throwing motion. The put is measured in the same way as for the hammer throw (see p. 135). A relatively new putting style, known as the 'Rotational' technique, in which the athlete turns in the circle rather like a discus thrower, is slowly gaining in popularity.

The rules relating to no-throws are much the same in this event as for the hammer, except that the athlete may not touch the top of the stopboard at any stage of the put. Also, the rules governing the competition itself are almost identical to those applied to the hammer event (see p. 136).

Because of the comparatively simple technical nature of

Gliding across the throwing circle, the good shot putter will be seen to generate great speed and explosive power to achieve the maximum possible throwing distance.

the shot put competitors are less likely to commit no-throws and may, therefore, produce their biggest throws at any point in the competition, although where only the best eight putters are going to get the full complement of trials, a good throw in the first three rounds is essential.

The greatest strength in male shot putting is concentrated in the United States and the Eastern bloc countries but on the women's side the East European stranglehold is total. The men's shot world record remained in American hands from 1934 to 1976 and only twice did the men's Olympic shot title go to non-Americans prior to 1972. In the women's shot the world record and Olympic title have remained East European property since 1948 and 1952, respectively. Puts of over 20.00 m (65 ft 7½ in) are expected of top international male performers, whilst their female counterparts regularly surpass 19.00 m (62 ft 4 in). Shot putting standards in the UK are relatively low with only a handful of male athletes topping 17.50 m (57 ft 5 in) and a few women achieving in excess of 16.00 m (52 ft 6 in).

Beyer, Udo (GDR): Born 9.8.1955. The dominant figure in men's shot putting for several years, he won the Olympic title in 1976 and took the gold medals at both the 1978 and 1982 European Championships. He also won the shot put at three European Cup finals and three World Cup events. He did, however, sustain defeats in major competition at the 1980 Olympic Games and the 1983 World Championships in which he placed third and sixth, respectively. He improved his world record during the latter year to 22.22 m (72 ft $10\frac{3}{4}$ in).

Helena Fibingerova (Czech)

Fibingerova, Helena (Czechoslovakia): Born 13.7.1949. The eternal bridesmaid of women's shot putting, she was five times runner-up to Ilona Slupianek in major competition. Her international honours include a third and two seconds at the European Championships of 1974, 1978 and 1982, respectively; an Olympic bronze medal in 1976; several European indoor titles; and two world records, the second of 22.32 m (73 ft $2\frac{3}{4}$ in), set in 1977. Her finest performance came in 1983 when at the age of 34 she finally defeated Slupianek to capture the women's world shot put title in Helsinki, throwing 21.05 m (69 ft $0\frac{3}{4}$ in).

Head, Venissa (UK): Born 1.9.1956. Primarily responsible for pioneering the greatest advance in British women's shot putting standards for many years, she followed up a UK record of 17.84 m (58 ft $6\frac{1}{2}$ in) in 1981 with the first 18 metres plus put by a British female, reaching 18.34 m (60 ft 2 in) indoors in 1983. Later, at the World Championships, she placed a very respectable 10th in the shot final producing the longest put ever achieved by a British woman in major competition of 18.41 m (60 ft 4¾ in).

Sarul, Edward (Poland): Born 16.11.1958. Having placed no higher than 11th at the 1982 European Championships, he greatly improved in 1983 to rank fifth among the main contenders for the shot put at the World Championships. Against all the odds he produced a 21.39 m (70 ft 2¼ in) put in the last round in Helsinki to take the world title. He quickly confirmed his world champion status with a second major victory in the European Cup final two weeks later.

Slupianek, Ilona (GDR): Born 24.9.1956. Arguably the most outstanding female shot putter ever, she won every major competition that she took part in from 1977 to 1982, including the 1978 and 1982 European Championships, the 1980 Olympic Games, three European Cup finals, three World Cup events and the 1979 World Student Games. That five-year period included a 12 month suspension for taking anabolic steroids but she was reinstated just in time to win the first of her European shot put titles. She also set world records of 22.36 m (73 ft 4½ in) and 22.45 m (73 ft 8 in) in 1980.

Winch, Mike (UK): Born 20.7.1948. Ranked second only to shot put record holder Geoff Capes among British throwers during his career, he has thrown further than any other Briton bar Capes, having reached his best ever distance of 20.43 m (67 ft 0½ in) in 1974. His outstanding international achievements include silver medal winning efforts at both the 1974 and 1982 Commonwealth Games.

Udo Beyer (GDR)

DISCUS THROW

A spectacular throwing event, the discus is very much in the territory of the strong man (and woman). Not quite as heavy as the average shot putter, the discus thrower tends to be taller with a more rangy, long-limbed build: the ideal physique for an event which requires both power and agility.

The discus itself is a disc-shaped implement, thicker at the centre than the edges, made of wood or plastic with a smooth metal rim. The men's discus weighs 2 kg (4.4 lb) with a diameter of 22 cm ($8\frac{3}{4}$ in); the women's discus is 1 kg (2.2 lb) and measures 18 cm ($7\frac{1}{4}$ in). The athlete throws the discus from a 2.5 m (8 ft $2\frac{1}{2}$ in) diameter circle which is partially enclosed by a protective cage, like that used in the hammer event. The discus must land within the standard 40° sector.

Strictly speaking, the event rules do not restrict the competitors to any particular throwing style but, in practice, a $1\frac{3}{4}$ turn technique will be seen to predominate. Standing at the rear of the circle, facing away from the throwing direction, the athlete grips the rim of the discus with his fingertips (some throwers apply turpentine to their hands to improve grip), performing one or two preliminary swings with the throwing arm before beginning to turn in the circle. Shifting his bodyweight on to one leg the thrower gyrates across the circle, swinging the discus around at arm's length as fast as possible. Turning towards the landing sector for the second time the thrower braces himself and whips the discus away in a wide swinging motion, spinning it at the moment of release to give it stability in flight. The sector markings give the spectators a good idea of the distance thrown but since the discus tends to slide on landing, particularly on wet grass, the judges have to watch where it first makes contact with the ground, measuring the throwing distance from that point.

Competition rules governing the number of throws each competitor may have, the factors invalidating a throw, and the method by which a tie is resolved, are all basically the same as for the shot put and hammer events and, of course, the competitor achieving the greatest throwing distance wins.

Rain can adversely affect all throwing events utilizing a circle, for a wet throwing surface becomes slippery, making it difficult for the thrower to maintain balance. Windy weather,

The discus thrower requires a fine sense of balance and perfect co-ordination, turning smoothly and quickly in the circle before launching the discus at precisely the right angle.

on the other hand, can work in the discus thrower's favour, adding several metres to the overall throwing distance if the implement is cast into a wind blowing not directly towards the thrower but from a slight angle (known as a 'quartering wind').

The experienced discus thrower will make relatively few no-throws in competition and will rarely produce the biggest throw of his series in the first round, using that initial trial to get the 'feel' of the throwing conditions and to register a valid opening throw.

Top-flight international male throwers would be expected to achieve upwards of 65.00 m (213 ft 3 in), whilst the best female throwers (the majority of whom are East Europeans) reaching distances in excess of 62.50 m (205 ft) would be of comparable standard. The generally mediocre UK throwing event standards also include the discus, in which relatively few leading British male and female throwers exceed 55.00 m (180 ft 5 in) and 50.00 m (164 ft), respectively.

Bugar, Imrich (Czechoslovakia): Born 14.4.1955. The most underrated of the world's leading throwers, few anticipated his victory in the discus at the 1982 European Championships, despite his 1980 Olympic second place and bronze medal winning effort at the earlier 1978 European Championships. He did not throw over 70 metres until 1983 (70.72 m/232 ft 0 in) but maintained his superb major competition consistency at the World Championships, throwing 67.72 m (222 ft 2 in) to secure the gold medal and take his place among the élite in the history of this event.

Imrich Bugar (Czech)

Oerter, Al (USA): Born 19.9.1936. The most amazing athlete in the history of athletics, he won the discus gold medal at four consecutive Olympic Games, from 1956 to 1968, and in 1980, at the age of 43, produced a throw of 69.46 m (227 ft 11 in) to surpass anything previously achieved in his long career. He also won the Pan-American Games discus title in Chicago in 1959.

Opitz, Martina (GDR): Born 12.12.1960. Probably the next in a long line of consistently outstanding East German women discus throwers, she beat an impressive field at the 1983 World Championships, throwing 68.94 m (226 ft 2 in) to become the women's world discus champion in her first major international outing. She beat the other Helsinki medallists again during the women's European Cup final later the same month and ended her 1983 season with a best throw of 70.26 m (230 ft 6 in).

Maria Petkova (Bulgaria)

Petkova, Maria (Bulgaria): Born 3.11.1955. One of the most consistent of top international discus throwers, she has compiled an enviable competitive record at major events without actually winning a major title. She finished runner-up in the discus at two Olympics (1976 and 1980), the 1982 European Championships, and placed third at the 1983 World Championships. She did, however, achieve less significant victories at the World Student Games of 1975 and 1977 and during the 1981 European Cup final.

She consistently threw over 70 metres each year from 1980 to 1983 and set a world record of 71.80 m (235 ft 7 in) in 1980.

Ritchie, Meg (UK): Born 6.7.1952. The first British women's discus thrower of real world class, she set a Commonwealth discus record of 67.48 m (221 ft 5 in) in 1981, almost 10 metres further than the next best throw by a Briton. She won her first major title in 1982 at the Commonwealth Games with a throw of 62.98 m (206 ft 7 in), her longest in major competition, and placed eighth at the World Championships in 1983, during which year she also set a UK women's shot record of 18.99 m (62 ft 3¾ in).

Slaney, Richard (UK): Born 16.5.1956. The top UK discus thrower in 1982 and 1983, he threw 64.64 m (212 ft 1 in) in the former year to exceed the UK record by 32 cm, but the performance was never ratified as a new national mark. He narrowly failed to win his first major championship medal at the 1982 Commonwealth Games, throwing just 20 cm short of the bronze medal winning mark.

JAVELIN THROW

Differing in several respects from the other throws, the javelin is in fact the only true throwing event in athletics. The international-class javelin thrower is generally less heavily built than the rest of the throwing fraternity, although he still needs to be strong with a fast, powerful throwing arm.

Unlike the other throwing events the javelin requires the athlete to throw from a runway, towards a relatively narrow 29° sector. The spear-like javelin consists of a metal or wooden shaft with a pointed metal head and a cord-bound handgrip. The men's implement is 2.7 m (8 ft 10½ in) long and weighs 800 g (28 oz), whilst the smaller women's javelin measures 2.3 m (7 ft 6½ in), weighing 600 g (21 oz).

The thrower's run-up, though not a full-out sprint, must be accurately judged so that the athlete does not overstep the curved scratch line at the end of the runway, thereby invalidating the throw. In the first ten strides the javelin is held horizontally above the shoulder. Then, in the last few strides, the thrower draws the javelin back to arm's length and, approaching the scratch line on the final stride, whips the implement forwards, throwing overarm, whilst attempting to release it on exactly the right trajectory. Most important, the javelin has to land point first for the throw to be valid, although it does not have to stick in. The throw is measured from the scratch line to the nearest mark made by the javelin point.

The rules governing the javelin throwing style, unlike those for the other throwing events, are very precise, stipulating that the implement must be *thrown* overarm and not released in any unorthodox style (such as slinging or hurling). Another stipulation, that the thrower must not face away from the sector before the javelin is released, is specifically designed to discourage unorthodox styles. All other basic rules relating to the competition are virtually identical to those applying to the other throwing events.

The majority of no-throws with the javelin result from the implement being inaccurately flighted, so that the javelin fails to strike the ground point first. Alternatively, where the javelin has been launched too high or too low, causing it to fall short, the thrower may be seen deliberately to invalidate the poor throw, by overstepping the scratch line, so as to save the officials the

Bracing the foremost leg on the final stride the thrower pulls the javelin through at tremendous speed, attempting to flight it accurately at the moment of release.

trouble of measuring the throw. The javelin's angle of trajectory on release is all-important if the best advantage is to be taken of the implement's aerodynamic design. The thrower also needs to take into account the wind direction when throwing, for a perfect launch into a headwind will carry the javelin considerably further than a throw executed in calm conditions.

Nothing short of an 85.00 m (278 ft 10 in) throwing potential would qualify a male athlete as a leading international javelin exponent, compared to a good international class performance for women of 61.00 m (201 ft 1 in). Among UK men anything over 75.00 m (246 ft 1 in) could be considered of the highest national standard. In contrast, a handful of British girls are of, or close to, good international standard, although strength in depth is lacking and anything over 50.00 m (164 ft 0 in) would be considered of good national standard.

Tina Lillak (Finland)

Michel, Detlef (GDR): Born 13.10.1955. Not always the most consistent of throwers he excelled at the 1983 World Championships beating American world record holder Tom Petranoff, among others, to capture the inaugural javelin world title. He also equalled the European record of 96.72 m (317 ft 4 in) that year, yet his earlier career had been somewhat patchy. He didn't qualify for the 1980 Olympic final and placed only third at the 1982 European Championships, despite being the favourite. In between, he won the javelin event at the European Cup final and placed second in the World Cup in 1981.

Lillak, Tina (Finland): Born 15.4.1961. Despite Finland's fine tradition in men's javelin, that country had not produced a female thrower of note until this girl came along. Smashing the world record out of the blue in 1982 with 72.40 m (237 ft 6 in), she disappointed at the European Championships in Athens, placing only fourth, but bounced back to take the gold medal at the 1983 World Championships in Helsinki, by virtue of a final round throw of 70.82 m (232 ft 4 in). She again smashed the world record in 1983, throwing 74.76 m (245 ft 3 in).

Ottley, Dave (UK): Born 5.8.1955. Although not quite fulfilling the potential demonstrated by his silver medal winning performance at the World Student Games of 1977, he did break the UK javelin record in 1980, throwing 85.52 m (280 ft 7 in). His major championship results since 1977 have, on the whole, been disappointing but he did well to place 4th in his event at both the 1979 and 1983 European Cup finals.

Petranoff, Tom (USA): Born 8.4.1958. The first American to have set a men's javelin world record in the past 24 years, he came within a whisker of breaking the 100 metres barrier when he reached 99.72 m (327 ft 2 in) in 1983. The favourite for the men's javelin title at the inaugural World Championships, he eventually finished runner-up, throwing far short of his world record with 85.60 m (280 ft 10 in).

Verouli, Anna (Greece): Born 13.11.1956. After placing no higher than 11th at the 1981 World Student Games, she improved out of all recognition in 1982 producing her first 70 metres throw (70.02 m/229 ft 9 in), on home ground in Athens, to win the final of the European Championships women's javelin and become the first Greek woman to win a medal in the history of those championships. A tough major championship temperament also earned her the javelin bronze medal at the 1983 World Championships.

Whitbread, Fatima (UK): Born 3.3.1961. One of the most exciting British female field event talents since Mary

Detlef Michel (GDR)

Rand, she went to the 1983 World Championships as a possible women's javelin finalist and came away with the silver medal, throwing 69.14 m (226 ft 10 in). Her European Junior Championship win in 1979 gave an indication of things to come, although competition nerves demoted her to third place at the 1982 Commonwealth Games in a competition that she was favourite to win. Shortly after the World Championships she won her first major senior event, throwing 69.04 m (226 ft 6 in) during the European Cup final.

DECATHLON & HEPTATHLON

Known as the multi-events, the men's decathlon and women's heptathlon are competitions, held over two consecutive days, to find the best all-round male and female athletes.

The decathlon consists of 10 separate events as follows:

Day 1: 100 m; long jump; shot put; high jump; 400 m
Day 2: 110 m hurdles; discus; pole vault; javelin; 1500 m

In the case of the women's seven-event heptathlon the composition is:

Day 1: 100 m hurdles; high jump; shot put; 200 m
Day 2: long jump; javelin; 800 m

As indicated, five separate events are contested on each day of the decathlon, whilst four are held on the first day of the heptathlon with the remainder on day 2. In both competitions the various constituent events are always contested in the same sequence over the two-day period.

Naturally, the multi-event specialist must possess a diverse range of athletic skills and abilities, combining the speed of a sprinter with the strength of a thrower, whilst retaining the hurdler's suppleness and the jumper's agility. To acquire these attributes the multi-events athlete has to train harder and longer than any other. However, because of this extreme diversity it would be impossible for even the most talented decathlete, or heptathlete, to achieve a level of performance in every event equal to that of the best individual event

specialists, but it is not unusual to find that most multi-event athletes excel in at least one of the individual events. In fact, the majority of the most successful all-rounders began their athletics careers specializing in an individual event.

The winner of a multi-events competition is decided not by how many events an athlete places first in but by a total points score accumulated during the competition. A competitor is awarded points for his best performance in each event, as calculated by reference to scoring tables produced by the IAAF. The better the performance, the higher the score achieved. For instance, a decathlon 100 metres clocking of 10.90 sec. would be worth 829 points, whereas a time of 11.00 sec. would score only 804 points. It would, therefore, be quite feasible for an athlete to achieve the highest overall points score in a competition without actually placing first in any one of the individual events. The scoring tables allow for a maximum possible score in a single event of approximately 1200 points, although in practice such a score would require a performance equal to—or even superior to—the existing world record for that event, which would be most unlikely.

In the event of two or more competitors producing identical total scores, the better overall position is awarded to the athlete who has placed higher in the majority of the events or, failing that, the one who has recorded the highest score in a single event during the competition.

Competition rules relating to the multi-events are basically

the same as for the individual events. The only differences are that in all track races each competitor is permitted two false starts without disqualification and in the throws and long jump only three trials per athlete are allowed. If an athlete fails to register a performance in any event during the competition, having perhaps committed three false starts on the track or three no-throws or jumps on the field, he does not score in that event. An athlete may continue in the competition after such a result but will certainly have lost any chance of winning, especially against international-class opposition. If an athlete actually fails to start an event he is automatically disqualified from the competition.

The multi-events invariably attract large fields, which make it necessary to stage heats in all the track races. In the 800 and 1500 metres, one or the other of which serves as the final competition event, the heats are composed so that the leading five or six competitors to that point can compete head-on for the final placings. Also, because several events have to be completed in one day, there is a time factor. Therefore, where a stadium has more than one set of jumps runways and high jump fans the competitors are split into two groups, or pools, for the jumps, competing simultaneously to save time.

Because of the length of a multi-events competition it is of paramount importance that the athletes should rest as much as possible whilst waiting to compete and, at the same time, stay warm to avoid muscle injuries. It is not unusual, therefore,

to see various competitors relaxing in sleeping bags or wrapped in blankets during the competition.

Where world records are concerned rules relating to wind-assisted performances in individual events also apply to the multi-events, i.e. if, for example, a sprint time is achieved with the aid of a following wind in excess of 4 m/sec. during a multi-events competition (the limit for individual events is 2 m/sec.), any resulting total points score bettering the existing world record would not qualify as a new record.

As often happens in major international championships, the multi-events tend to be overshadowed when conducted at the same time as certain individual events. Nevertheless, many spectators will discover that for them the decathlon and heptathlon are perhaps the most fascinating and absorbing of all athletics contests.

Decathlon: To be able to handle such a demanding combination of events the decathlete obviously needs to be strong, though not too heavily built, and because of the sequence of these events the sprinter/jumper types tend to fare better than their throws-orientated rivals on the first day; the latter come into their own more on the second day.

In most cases the decathlete will score more points during the first day's competition than the second, for events such as the 1500 metres and pole vault create difficulties for many competitors, whilst the fatigue and stiffness carried over from

day 1 must adversely affect the second day's performances to some degree. The final event, the 1500 metres, is traditionally the decathlete's weakest event, earning the least number of points. This is because the competitors are both physically and mentally drained by the time they come to the last event.

Ideally, the decathlete should have no real weakness in any event. To register a top-class score he would need to average at least 800 points per event, which would require the following performances:

Day 1
100 m: 11.01 sec.
LJ: 6.90 m (22 ft 7¾ in)
SP: 15.19 m (49 ft 10 in)
HJ: 1.94 m (6 ft 4½ in)
400 m: 50.1 sec.

Day 2
110 m hurdles: 15.47 sec.
DT: 45.99 m (150 ft 10 in)
PV: 3.98 m (13 ft 0¾ in)
JT: 63.17 m (207 ft 3 in)
1500 m: 4 min. 02.0 sec.

Apart from Daley Thompson, Britain has not produced any really outstanding decathletes and, nowadays, anything over a score of 7,200 points would place a UK all-rounder among the best in the country.

Heptathlon: The seven-event heptathlon was introduced in 1981 to replace the five-event pentathlon, which tended to favour the lighter, faster girls as it included only one throwing event. The introduction of the javelin for the heptathlon has

now placed more emphasis on strength, so the present-day heptathlete is generally bigger and more powerful.

The event sequence in the heptathlon gives quite an even balance over the two days of competition, therefore no particular type of athlete is favoured more than any other on one day but, as in the decathlon, the heptathlete cannot afford to have a significant weakness. The top international heptathlete would need to average in the region of 875 points per event to come up with a good-class score of 6125 points and to achieve that score the level of performance necessary in each event would be as follows:

Day 1
100 m hurdles: 13.93 sec.
SP: 14.64 m (48 ft 0½ in)
HJ: 1.64 m (5 ft 4½ in)
200 m: 24.68 sec.

Day 2
LJ: 5.86 m (19 ft 3 in)
JT: 47.24 m (155 ft 0 in)
800 m: 2 min. 13.5 sec.

Despite the very recent introduction of the heptathlon, athletes from the Eastern bloc countries are already playing a leading role in the new event and are unlikely to relinquish their position in the near future. Heptathlon performances among UK athletes are currently of a good standard, with a number of the top girls scoring over 5500 points: a sign that progress in this event should be quite rapid in the next few years.

Frederick, Jane (USA): Born 7.4.1952. The world's leading heptathlete outside of Europe, she scored 6,458 points in 1982 to rank sixth on the all-time list but performed below par at the 1983 World Championships, eventually failing to complete the competition. She won the heptathlon's predecessor, the five event pentathlon, at the 1975 World Student Games but did not finish the Pan American Games pentathlon in 1979, forfeiting an almost certain victory.

Hingsen, Jurgen (FRG): Born 25.1.1958. Apparently destined always to finish second to Daley Thompson, this colossal West German (height: 2.00 m /6 ft 7 in, weight: 97 kg/213 lb) has twice relieved the Englishman of the world record, scoring 8,723 points in 1982 and 8,777 in 1983, but has yet to beat him in competition. A superb decathlete nonetheless, he placed third in the 1977 European Junior Championships and finished runner-up in both the 1982 European Championships and 1983 World Championships competitions.

Livermore, Judy (UK): Born 14.11.1960. Fast approaching top world class in the heptathlon, she is particularly strong in the first two events, the 100 metres hurdles and high jump, but is, as yet, weak in the second day's events. She placed 7th at the 1982 European Championships, setting a Commonwealth record of 6,286 points, and finished runner-up in that year's Commonwealth Games. In 1983 she lead the World Championships heptathlon after three events but failed to register a valid throw in the javelin. She finished the season on a high note, however, recording a new Commonwealth record score of 6,353 points.

Ramona Neubert (GDR)

Neubert, Ramona (GDR): Born 26.7.1958. Totally dominant in the heptathlon, she had broken the world record four times up to the end of 1983, her highest score totalling 6,836 points. Having finished just out of the medals in the pentathlon at the 1980 Olympic Games, she immediately took to the new event, comfortably winning the European and world heptathlon titles in 1982 and 1983, respectively. Although good all-round her strongest event is the long jump, in which she achieved a superb wind-assisted 7.00 m (22 ft 11¾ in) jump in 1981.

Thompson, Daley (UK): Born 30.7.1958. He is indisputably the greatest decathlete that ever lived and now holds a unique collection of Commonwealth (1978 and 1982), European (1982), Olympic (1980) and World (1983) decathlon titles. His only defeat in major competition, since his 1977 European Junior Championship success, came at the 1978 European Championships, where as a 20-year-old he finished second to Russian Aleksandr Grebenyuk. He had also broken the world record three times by the end of 1983, his highest score being 8,743 points (1982).

Voss, Torsten (GDR): Born 24.3.1963. A possible decathlon star of the future, he was runner-up in the 1981 European Junior Championships but the following year scored 8,387 points to smash Daley Thompson's world junior record by a huge 263 points margin. He did not complete the European Championships decathlon in 1982 but at the World Championships the following year did exceptionally well to finish in sixth place, having occupied the bronze medal position after five events.

Daley Thompson (UK)

CROSS-COUNTRY RUNNING

During the winter months, when it is too cold and wet for track athletics, the cross-country season gets under way. One of the oldest athletics pursuits, cross-country running, practised both by men and women, is a form of long distance running over the country taking in terrain such as fields, woodland and parkland. The sport attracts mainly long distance and middle distance runners, who participate both for the competition and to maintain stamina and fitness with the summer season in mind.

A typical cross-country course consists of several laps of a circuit of perhaps 3–5 km (2–3 miles) around, which is marked out with flags and arrows to keep the runners on the correct course. Cross-country races are usually contested as team events in which maybe the first four finishers out of six runners representing a particular team score points in the race equivalent to their actual finishing positions, i.e. the race winner scores one point, the runner-up scores two points, and so on. Therefore the winning team is the one with the lowest points score. Team relay races are also quite popular, with one member of each team running one lap (leg) of the course and executing the changeover by touching the hand of the next runner in line. The finishing area of a cross-country race is generally roped off to form a narrow channel (funnel) which the finishing runners can only enter one at a time. Since dozens of runners may cross the finish line in a matter of seconds the funnel system ensures that the runners are placed in the correct finishing order.

Cross-country running English-style is undoubtedly the most demanding in the world. The typical English course is long—up to 14.5 km (9 miles) for men and 6 km (4 miles) for women—and extremely arduous, including hills, ploughland, streams and invariably, on the flat stretches, thick mud. On the Continent of Europe, where cross-country has a large following, the courses tend to be shorter, flatter and faster with a number of artificial obstacles, rather like the steeple-chase on the track. These Continental courses—often run on horse racing circuits—tend to favour the faster middle distance

The true cross-country course, such as the typical English variety, incorporates all kinds of terrain and obstacles, including woods, hills, fields and, as shown here, even the occasional stream.

track athletes, whereas English courses are more the preserve of the strong, stamina-orientated long distance track and road runners.

The cross-country season in England, which commences in October and probably stretches over a longer period than in any other country, reaches its climax with the National Cross-Country Championships. The women's and men's championship races are held separately in February and March, respectively. So popular are these championships that the senior men's race, traditionally held over a standard imperial distance of 9 miles (14.5 km), attracts close to 2000 starters. The metrically-measured senior women's courses vary from year to year but rarely exceed 6 km (4 miles).

Annual World-Cross Country Championships, under IAAF jurisdiction, are held at the end of March and although the courses are of the Continental type, English teams have invariably excelled in these races. The senior men's race is over a standard 12 km (8 mile) distance but the women may run anything from 4–5 km (2½–3 miles). There is also a junior men's race over 7–8 km (4½–5 miles).

Clarke, Dave (UK): Born 1.1.1958. One of the most outstanding British cross-country runners in recent years, he won the English National cross-country Championships in 1982 and finished second in the same event in both 1981 and 1983. In the IAAF World Cross-Country Championships he finished 9th in 1982 and 7th in 1983, just 13 seconds behind the winner Bekele Debele. He is also an accomplished track runner and ran his first sub-4 minute mile (3:56.95) and first sub-28 minutes 10 km (27:55.7) in 1982.

Bekele Debele (Ethiopia)

Puica, Maricica (Romania): Born 29.7.1950. Primarily a track runner and women's mile world record setter with 4:17.44 in 1982, she became the first woman to beat the great Norwegian female distance star, Grete Waitz, in a cross-country race when she relieved her of the women's IAAF World Cross-Country title in 1982. Also a top 3000 metres runner on the track, the Romanian took the silver medal over that distance at both the indoor and outdoor European Championships in 1982.

Debele, Bekele (Ethiopia): Born c. 1963. One of the biggest surprises in the history of the IAAF World Cross-Country Championships was the victory of this 20-year-old African distance runner in the 1983 senior men's race. In only his second year of athletics he took on and beat the strongest international cross-country field ever assembled. In the previous year's championships he had been only the sixth Ethiopian finisher in the junior race.

ROAD RUNNING

The runners in a road relay do not have to pass a baton from one to the other. The incoming runner only has to touch his team- mate's hand to send him on his way.

Road running in its earliest form even predates track and cross-country running, although until recent times it was one of the least developed branches of athletics. Road running is basically long distance running on roads and for many years road races were staged only in spring and autumn in the UK, filling in the gaps between the summer track season and winter cross-country season. However, such has been the recent growth and increase in worldwide popularity of this branch of athletics, that road running has now become a year-round pursuit.

Road races can vary greatly in length, from 2 or 3 miles to many hundreds of miles, but distances such as 5, 10 and 20 miles and 10 km are by far the most common, both for men and women. The types of course can vary also, including point-to-point and out and back courses covering several laps of a circuit. Road races are generally contested as team events making use of a points scoring system to decide the winning team, as in cross-country races (see p. 158). Road relay races between athletics club teams are another popular form of road running, particularly in the UK.

The new interest in road running has perhaps spread faster in the United States than anywhere else and as well as the numerous marathons and shorter road races under the jurisdiction of the USA's athletics governing body, the Athletics Congress, a professional road racing circuit organized by the Association of Road Racing Athletes, has also recently emerged. The Road Runners Club, formed in 1952, was mainly responsible for initially popularizing road running in Britain but it was the more recent jogging and marathon booms which swelled both domestic and overseas road race fields to several hundreds and even thousands.

The kind of running tactics employed in road races depend very much on the length of the race. At distances much over 16 km (10 miles) potential race winners will apply similar make-or-break tactics to those seen in a marathon. The shorter road races are more like long distance track events in that the race leaders may try to break away from the opposition by surging, whilst good finishing speed is also essential in a close race.

In the longer road races runners must guard against the dangers of dehydration and overheating in warm weather, taking regular drinks and using the wet sponges provided at the refreshment points.

One advantage that road running has over track running is that road race courses are more or less straight with few, if any, sharp turns, whereas the track runner has to negotiate two bends each lap. Consequently, flat road race courses are often 'faster' than the track and, therefore, the best road times over certain recognized distances are superior to the official track records for the same distances. There are no official records in road running as courses can vary considerably in nature.

The only road running event universally recognized as a national and major international championship distance is, of course, the marathon. Apart from the marathon the only other road races with national championship status in the UK are the annual 6 and 12-stage AAA National Road Relays, which are contested by teams from the top athletics clubs throughout Britain.

Rose, Nick (UK): Born 30.12.1951. An outstanding track and cross-country runner with a 1977 European Cup final 5000 metres win and a third place in the 1980 World Cross-Country Championships to his credit he has also produced some exceptional performances on the road. In 1979 he clocked 46 min. 37 sec. for 10 miles and reduced that time to one of the fastest ever recorded on the road of 46:04 in the USA two years later. His 10 km time of 27:43 in a New York road race in 1981 was thought to be a world best, but the course was later found to be short.

Nick Rose (UK)

Seko, Toshihiko (Japan): Born 15.7.1956. Although he did not compete in the 1980 Olympic or 1983 World Championships marathons, he is regarded as one of the world's top road runners. He ran one of the fastest ever marathon times in 1983, clocking 2:08:38 to win the Tokyo marathon, but perhaps his greatest achievement has been in notching up three straight wins in Japan's famous Fukuoka marathon from 1978 to 1980. He also set a course record of 2:09:26 during his 1981 Boston marathon win and the same year established a 30 km track world record of 1:29:18.8.

Waitz, Grete (Norway): Born 1.10.1953. In addition to her cross-country, track and marathon exploits (see Marathon: Personalities), she can also point to other outstanding achievements on the road. Her string of world best performances on the road include a 10 km time of 31 minutes dead, set in 1980 and nearly two minutes faster than the best women's track performance that year; a 10 miles best of 53.05 in 1979; and a half marathon timed at 1:09.19 in 1982.

ULTRA-LONG DISTANCE RUNNING

This branch of athletics is unquestionably the most demanding, which probably explains why it has a relatively small following. If nothing else, the ultra-long distance runner must possess phenomenal powers of endurance that can only be developed through clocking up high mileages in training.

Ultra-long distance running incorporates both track and road events of anything from around 48 km (30 miles) upwards and, in addition, there is a track race in which competitors endeavour to cover as much distance as possible during a 24-hour period. Since 1955 the IAAF has not recognized ultra-long distance track performances for world record purposes, although the Road Runners Club maintains its own unofficial record lists for track events over 30 km (18 miles). All of the standard ultra-long distance events run on the track are also contested on the road but whereas the stopwatch is probably the most important criterion on the track, the race itself becomes the prime concern on the roads.

Perhaps the most famous international ultra-long distance race is the Comrades Marathon, run annually in South Africa. This 88 km (54½ mile) race is run in opposite directions in alternate years, the toughest course being the Durban to Pietermaritzburg route which involves a gradual rise in altitude from sea level to 762 m (2500 ft). The inaugural Comrades Marathon was staged in 1921 and over the years has attracted many of the world's greatest ultra-long distance runners. The most popular ultra-long distance road race in the UK is the annual London to Brighton run. As long ago as 1837 a professional runner named John Townsend ran a 52¼ mile London to Brighton course in 8 h. 37 min., but today the top runners cover the course (which is now approximately 86 km (53½ miles) long) in close to 5 hours, averaging better than six minutes per mile all the way.

A recently revived ultra-long distance track event is the six day race which was popular more than 100 years ago. Here the object is to cover as much distance as possible during a 144-hour period, although the runners can leave the track whenever they wish to sleep or to take food. The first six day

Ultra distance runners are often quite stockily built, for sturdy limbs can better withstand the rigours of countless hours of steady running. Back-up teams provide the competitors with food, drink and much needed encouragement during their ordeal.

race this century was staged in the USA at Woodside, California, in July 1980, when American Don Choi covered 401 miles (645 m); a far cry from the 623 miles 1320 yards (just over 1000 m) clocked up by Briton George Littlewood in an event at Madison Square Garden, New York, in 1888.

Among the longest ultra distance races are the Trans American races that take place from time to time. One such race, staged in 1929 from New York to Los Angeles, was 3665 miles (5897 km) long, taking the winner some 79 days in all—an average of more than 46 miles (74 km) per day.

After dabbling for a number of years, women finally moved into the field of ultra-long distance running in the late 1960s and already they are producing some astonishing performances. For example, a French girl named Chantal Langlace recorded a time for 100 km (62 miles) on the road in 1980 which was faster than anything achieved by a male runner until as recently as 1970.

At the present time Britain and the United States are the super powers of ultra-long distance running, with athletes from those nations virtually dominating the unofficial record lists.

165

Dowdle, Dave (UK): Born 7.11.1954. As a relative youngster in this field of athletics he took the ultra distance running world by storm in 1982, covering a phenomenal 170 miles 1412 yards in a 24 hour track race to smash the world best performance during his début at the event. Moving up in distance the following year he also broke the 48 hour track world best, clocking up 238 miles 1122 yards and setting other new world marks at 300 km and 200 miles on other road-running occasions.

Ritchie, Don (UK): Born 6.7.1944. Of the seven recognized track and road ultra distance events up to and including 100 miles, he has held world best performances at six of them. An amazingly consistent performer in what is the toughest of athletics pursuits, he had failed in only one of his deliberate record attempts on the track prior to 1984, perhaps his finest performance being a 50 mile mark of 4 h. 51 min. 49 sec. in 1983. He also won the famous London to Brighton run in 1977 and 1978 and clocked a marathon best of 2:19:35 in 1983.

Don Ritchie (UK)

Watson, Leslie (UK): Born 4.2.1948. A prolific marathon and ultra distance runner, she competed in as many as 20 marathons during 1981, in which year she also set a world best mark of 6 h. 02 min. 37 sec. for 50 miles on the road. She set the inaugural women's London to Brighton race record of 6 h. 56 min. 10 sec. for the 54¼ mile course in 1980 and in 1983 smashed the 50 mile track world record with 6 h. 20 min. 42 sec.

INDOOR ATHLETICS

Although indoor athletics has existed since before the turn of the century it is only in recent years that it has developed into a major international winter sport. Indeed, it is the most suitable form of winter competition available to the sprinters, hurdlers, jumpers and some throwers who, unlike the distance runners, cannot fall back on cross-country and road running to maintain their competitive edge.

There is no such thing as a standard indoor athletics track, for the size of the track is very much dependent upon the dimensions of the indoor arena housing it. The majority of indoor tracks, particularly on the Continent, are four or five lane circuits of 200 metres in length but in the United States, where indoor athletics is perhaps more popular than anywhere else in the world, the numerous indoor tracks range from 352 yards to just 160 yards (11 laps to the mile) and even now the Americans still hold a number of their indoor races over imperial distances. The bends on these small tracks are extremely tight and have to be banked so that they can be negotiated at speed by the sprinters. The indoor tracks are usually wooden-based with synthetic rubberized surfaces, which give them similar properties to the outdoor all-weather tracks.

The nature of the indoor arena tends to restrict the number and type of events that can be effectively staged. For example, the straights of a 200 m indoor track are not long enough for short sprint races which, therefore, have to be run on a separate section of track situated on the infield of the main track, extending from just inside the top bend to the opposite bend. This section of track measures no more than 60 metres in length: the standard distance of the majority of the short sprints and hurdles races (only five flights of hurdles used) indoors. Because of the spacial confinement of indoor facilities the only throwing event which can be safely staged indoors is the shot put, but even in this event the implements have to be leather-covered so as not to damage the track. Similarly, it is simply not practical to stage events such as the 400 metres hurdles on a banked indoor track and although steeplechase events are held they do not include a water jump. In the flat 400 metres the first 200 m lap is run in lanes to avoid collisions which would inevitably occur in a sprint race of this nature, as runners jostled for the pole position on the inside lane. There are races for the distance runners but few are longer than 3000 metres, which is a standard major championship distance indoors.

Running on a small banked indoor track requires entirely different skills and tactics to those applying to outdoor running. It is virtually impossible for a runner to overtake rivals on the tight banked bends, whilst exceptional acceleration is needed to do so on the short straights. Running on a banked bend is an art in itself, which small runners find far easier than tall, long-striding athletes. Also, because of the relatively cramped conditions on an indoor track, there is often a good deal of bumping and boring during indoor races, so the seasoned competitor needs to be sufficiently robust to hold his ground in competition. In the short sprints the fast starter fares much better than the athlete who takes 40 or 50 metres to get into his rhythm. In the jumps the horizontal jumpers often have to make do with shorter runways, whereas the vertical jumpers have the advantage of competing in calm

conditions; indoors there are, of course, never the problems created by adverse weather conditions.

As a result of the lack of standardization from one indoor arena to another there are no official indoor records, only indoor best performances which, with one or two notable exceptions, are generally inferior to outdoor records for the same events. In addition, any indoor track performance set on a track longer than 200 metres or 220 yards cannot be recognized even as an indoor best.

The smaller size of indoor tracks and arenas brings the athletes and spectators much closer together, which makes for an electric atmosphere during competitions.

MISCELLANEOUS TRACK AND FIELD EVENTS

In addition to the standard events staged at all national and major international athletics championships there are a number of non-standard events, some of which have IAAF world record status, that quite often appear in competitions such as international invitation meetings.

Sprints

Non-standard sprint events include 300 and 600 metres distances for men and women, although only the former distance involves the use of starting blocks. There is also a 4 × 200 metres sprint relay which has official world record status for both sexes.

Middle distances

Track events of 1000, 2000 and 3000 metres are run by both men and women but whereas all three are IAAF world record events for men, only the longer distance is for women, for whom it is also a championship event. Two other frequently staged non-standard events are the 2 miles and the men's 2000 metres steeplechase. There are also two middle distance relays with IAAF world record status, namely the 4 × 800 and 4 × 1500 metres events, the latter distance yet to gain recognition as a women's event.

Long distances

Long distance track events such as 20, 25 and 30 km, plus the one hour run (for distance), are of too long a duration to include in a standard track and field events programme and would more likely be staged individually, as a centrepiece in a specially arranged meeting. Although each of these events is open to both men and women, they have IAAF world record status only for men.

Walking events

Timewise it would not be practical to include any of the longer men's and women's track walking events in a full track and field programme but distances such as 1500 metres or a mile, 3, 5 and 10 km are often staged. Of these just the women's 5 and 10 km distances are IAAF world record events.

RECORDS SECTION

Olympic Games
Track and field gold medallists

Men's events

100 metres		sec.
1896	T.E. Burke (USA)	12.0
1900	F.W. Jarvis (USA)	11.0
1904	A. Hahn (USA)	11.0
1908	R.E. Walker (S. A.)	10.8
1912	R.C. Craig (USA)	10.8
1920	C.W. Paddock (USA)	10.8
1924	H.M. Abrahams (GB)	10.6
1928	P. Williams (Canada)	10.8
1932	T.E. Tolan (USA)	10.3
1936	J.C. Owens (USA)	10.3
1948	W.H. Dillard (USA)	10.3
1952	L.J. Remigino (USA)	10.4
1956	B.J. Morrow (USA)	10.5
1960	A. Hary (Germany)	10.2
1964	R.L. Hayes (USA)	10.0
1968	J.R. Hines (USA)	9.95
1972	V. Borzov (USSR)	10.14
1976	H. Crawford (Trin.)	10.06
1980	A.W. Wells (GB)	10.25

200 metres		sec.
1900	J.W.B. Tewksbury (USA)	22.2
1904	A. Hahn (USA)	21.6
1908	R. Kerr (Canada)	22.6
1912	R.C. Craig (USA)	21.7
1920	A. Woodring (USA)	22.0
1924	J.V. Scholz (USA)	21.6
1928	P. Williams (Canada)	21.8
1932	T.E. Tolan (USA)	21.2
1936	J.C. Owens (USA)	20.7
1948	M.E. Patton (USA)	21.1
1952	A.W. Stanfield (USA)	20.7
1956	B.J. Morrow (USA)	20.6
1960	L. Berruti (Italy)	20.5
1964	H. Carr (USA)	20.3
1968	T.C. Smith (USA)	19.83
1972	V. Borzov (USSR)	20.00
1976	D. Quarrie (Jam.)	20.23
1980	P. Mennea (Italy)	20.19

400 metres		sec.
1896	T.E. Burke (USA)	54.2
1900	M.W. Long (USA)	49.4
1904	H.L. Hillman (USA)	49.2
1908	W. Halswelle (GB)	50.0
1912	C.D. Reidpath (USA)	48.2
1920	B.G.D. Rudd (S. A.)	49.6
1924	E.H. Liddell (GB)	47.6
1928	R.J. Barbuti (USA)	47.8
1932	W.A. Carr (USA)	46.2
1936	A.F. Williams (USA)	46.5
1948	A.S. Wint (Jam.)	46.2
1952	A.G. Rhoden (Jam.)	45.9
1956	C.L. Jenkins (USA)	46.7
1960	O.C. Davis (USA)	44.9
1964	M.D. Larrabee (USA)	45.1
1968	L. Evans (USA)	43.86
1972	V. Matthews (USA)	44.66
1976	A. Juantorena (Cuba)	44.26
1980	V. Markin (USSR)	44.60

800 metres		min. sec.
1896	E.H. Flack (Aus.)	2 11.0
1900	A.E. Tysoe (GB)	2 01.2
1904	J.D. Lightbody (USA)	1 56.0
1908	M.W. Sheppard (USA)	1 52.8
1912	J.E. Meredith (USA)	1 51.9
1920	A.G. Hill (GB)	1 53.4
1924	D.G.A. Lowe (GB)	1 52.4
1928	D.G.A. Lowe (GB)	1 51.8
1932	T. Hampson (GB)	1 49.7
1936	J.Y. Woodruff (USA)	1 52.9
1948	M.G. Whitfield (USA)	1 49.2
1952	M.G. Whitfield (USA)	1 49.2
1956	T.W. Courtney (USA)	1 47.7
1960	P.G. Snell (N. Z.)	1 46.3
1964	P.G. Snell (N. Z.)	1 45.1
1968	R. Doubell (Aus.)	1 44.3
1972	D. Wottle (USA)	1 45.9
1976	A. Juantorena (Cuba)	1 43.5
1980	S.M.J. Ovett (GB)	1 45.4

1500 metres		min. sec.
1896	E.H. Flack (Aus.)	4 33.2
1900	C. Bennett (GB)	4 06.2
1904	J.D. Lightbody (USA)	4 05.4
1908	M.W. Sheppard (USA)	4 03.4
1912	A.N.S. Jackson (GB)	3 56.8
1920	A.G. Hill (GB)	4 01.8
1924	P.J. Nurmi (Fin.)	3 53.6
1928	H.E. Larva (Fin.)	3 53.2
1932	L. Beccali (Italy)	3 51.2

1936	J.E. Lovelock (N. Z.)	3	47.8
1948	H. Eriksson (Swe.)	3	49.8
1952	J. Barthel (Lux.)	3	45.1
1956	R.M. Delany (Ire.)	3	41.2
1960	H.J. Elliot (Aus.)	3	35.6
1964	P.G. Snell (N. Z.)	3	38.1
1968	K. Keino (Kenya)	3	34.9
1972	P. Vasala (Fin.)	3	36.3
1976	J. Walker (N. Z.)	3	39.2
1980	S.N. Coe (GB)	3	38.4

5000 metres
		min.	sec.
1912	H. Kolehmainen (Fin.)	14	36.6
1920	J. Guillemot (Fr.)	14	55.6
1924	P.J. Nurmi (Fin.)	14	31.2
1928	V.J. Ritola (Fin.)	14	38.0
1932	L.A. Lehtinen (Fin.)	14	30.0
1936	G. Hockert (Fin.)	14	22.2
1948	G.E.G. Reiff (Belg.)	14	17.6
1952	E. Zatopek (Czech.)	14	06.6
1956	V. Kuts (USSR)	13	39.6
1960	M.G. Halberg (N. Z.)	13	43.4
1964	R.K. Schul (USA)	13	48.8
1968	M. Gammoudi (Tun.)	14	05.0
1972	L. Viren (Fin.)	13	26.4
1976	L. Viren (Fin.)	13	24.8
1980	M. Yifter (Eth.)	13	21.0

10,000 metres
		min.	sec.
1912	H. Kolehmainen (Fin.)	31	20.8
1920	P.J. Nurmi (Fin.)	31	45.8
1924	V.J. Ritola (Fin.)	30	23.2
1928	P.J. Nurmi (Fin.)	30	18.8
1932	J. Kusocinski (Pol.)	30	11.4
1936	I. Salminen (Fin.)	30	15.4
1948	E. Zatopek (Czech.)	29	59.6
1952	E. Zatopek (Czech.)	29	17.0
1956	V. Kuts (USSR)	28	45.6
1960	P. Bolotnikov (USSR)	28	32.2
1964	W.M. Mills (USA)	28	24.4
1968	M. Temu (Kenya)	29	27.4
1972	L. Viren (Fin.)	27	38.4
1976	L. Viren (Fin.)	27	40.4
1980	M. Yifter (Eth.)	27	42.7

Marathon
		h.	min.	sec.
1896	S. Louis (Greece)	2	58	50.0
1900	M. Theato (Fr.)	2	59	45.0
1904	T.J. Hicks (USA)	3	28	53.0
1908	J.J. Hayes (USA)	2	55	18.4
1912	K.K. McArthur (S.A.)	2	36	54.8
1920	H. Kolehmainen (Fin.)	2	32	35.8
1924	A. O. Stenroos (Fin.)	2	41	22.6

1928	B.M. El Ouafi (France)			
		2	32	57.0
1932	J.C. Zabala (Arg.)	2	31	36.0
1936	K. Son (Japan)	2	29	19.2
1948	D. Cabrera (Arg.)	2	34	51.6
1952	E. Zatopek (Czech.)	2	23	03.2
1956	A. Mimoun (Fr.)	2	25	00.0
1960	Abebe Bikila (Eth.)	2	15	16.2
1964	Abebe Bikila (Eth.)	2	12	11.2
1968	M. Wolde (Eth.)	2	20	26.4
1972	F. Shorter (USA)	2	12	19.8
1976	W. Cierpinski (GDR)	2	09	55.0
1980	W. Cierpinski (GDR)	2	11	03.0

3000 metres steeplechase
		min.	sec.
1920	P. Hodge (GB)	10	00.4
1924	V.J. Ritola (Fin.)	9	33.6
1928	T.A. Loukola (Fin.)	9	21.8
1932	V. Iso-Hollo (Fin.)	10	33.4
1936	V. Iso-Hollo (Fin.)	9	03.8
1948	T. Sjostrand (Swe.)	9	04.6
1952	H. Ashenfelter (USA)	8	45.4
1956	C.W. Brasher (GB)	8	41.2
1960	Z. Krzyszkowiak (Pol.)	8	34.2
1964	G. Roelants (Belg.)	8	30.8
1968	A. Biwott (Kenya)	8	51.0
1972	K. Keino (Kenya)	8	23.6
1976	A. Garderud (Swe.)	8	08.0
1980	B. Malinowski (Pol.)	8	09.7

110 metres hurdles
		sec.
1896	T.P. Curtis (USA)	17.6
1900	A.C. Kraenzlein (USA)	15.4
1904	F.W. Schule (USA)	16.0
1908	F.C. Smithson (USA)	15.0
1912	F.W. Kelly (USA)	15.1
1920	E.J. Thomson (Canada)	14.8
1924	D.C. Kinsey (USA)	15.0
1928	S.J.M. Atkinson (S.A.)	14.8
1932	G.J. Saling (USA)	14.6
1936	F.G. Towns (USA)	14.2
1948	W.F. Porter (USA)	13.9
1952	W.H. Dillard (USA)	13.7
1956	L.Q. Calhoun (USA)	13.5
1960	L.Q. Calhoun (USA)	13.8
1964	H.W. Jones (USA)	13.6
1968	W. Davenport (USA)	13.33
1972	R. Milburn (USA)	13.24
1976	G. Drut (Fr.)	13.30
1980	T. Munkelt (GDR)	13.39

400 metres hurdles
		sec.
1900	J.W.B. Tewksbury (USA)	57.6

1904	H.L. Hillman (USA)	53.0
1908	C.J. Bacon (USA)	55.0
1920	F.F. Loomis (USA)	54.0
1924	F.M. Taylor (USA)	52.6
1928	Lord Burghley (GB)	53.4
1932	R.M.N. Tisdall (Ire.)	51.7
1936	G.F. Hardin (USA)	52.4
1948	R.V. Cochran (USA)	51.1
1952	C.H. Moore (USA)	50.8
1956	G.A. Davis (USA)	50.1
1960	G.A. Davis (USA)	49.3
1964	W.J. Cawley (USA)	49.6
1968	D.P. Hemery (GB)	48.12
1972	J. Akii-Bua (Uganda)	47.82
1976	E. Moses (USA)	47.64
1980	V. Beck (GDR)	48.70

4 × 100 metres relay

		sec.
1912	Great Britain	42.4
1920	United States	42.2
1924	United States	41.0
1928	United States	41.0
1932	United States	40.0
1936	United States	39.8
1948	United States	40.6
1952	United States	40.1
1956	United States	39.5
1960	Germany	39.5
1964	United States	39.0
1968	United States	38.23
1972	United States	38.19
1976	United States	38.33
1980	USSR	38.26

4 × 400 metres relay

		min. sec.
1912	United States	3 16.6
1920	Great Britain	3 22.2
1924	United States	3 16.0
1928	United States	3 14.2
1932	United States	3 08.2
1936	Great Britain	3 09.0
1948	United States	3 10.4
1952	Jamaica	3 03.9
1956	United States	3 04.7
1960	United States	3 02.2
1964	United States	3 00.7
1968	United States	2 56.1
1972	Kenya	2 59.8
1976	United States	2 58.7
1980	USSR	3 01.1

High jump

		metres
1896	E.H. Clark (USA)	1.81

1900	I.K. Baxter (USA)	1.90
1904	S.S. Jones (USA)	1.80
1908	H.F. Porter (USA)	1.90
1912	A.W. Richards (USA)	1.93
1920	R.W. Landon (USA)	1.93
1924	H.M. Osborn (USA)	1.98
1928	R.W. King (USA)	1.94
1932	D. McNaughton (Canada)	1.97
1936	C.C. Johnson (USA)	2.03
1948	J.A. Winter (Aus.)	1.98
1952	W.F. Davis (USA)	2.04
1956	C.E. Dumas (USA)	2.12
1960	R. Shavlakadze (USSR)	2.16
1964	V. Brumel (USSR)	2.18
1968	R. Fosbury (USA)	2.24
1972	J. Tarmak (USSR)	2.23
1976	J. Wszola (Pol.)	2.25
1980	G. Wessig (GDR)	2.36

Pole vault

		metres
1896	W.W. Hoyt (USA)	3.30
1900	I.K. Baxter (USA)	3.30
1904	C.E. Dvorak (USA)	3.50
1908	E.T. Cooke (USA) and A.C. Gilbert (USA)	3.71
1912	H.S. Babcock (USA)	3.95
1920	F.K. Foss (USA)	4.09
1924	L.S. Barnes (USA)	3.95
1928	S.W. Carr (USA)	4.20
1932	W.W. Miller (USA)	4.31
1936	E.E. Meadows (USA)	4.35
1948	O.G. Smith (USA)	4.30
1952	R.E. Richards (USA)	4.55
1956	R.E. Richards (USA)	4.56
1960	D.G. Bragg (USA)	4.70
1964	F.M. Hansen (USA)	5.10
1968	R. Seagren (USA)	5.40
1972	W. Nordwig (GDR)	5.50
1976	T. Slusarski (Pol.)	5.50
1980	W. Kozakiwwicz (Pol.)	5.78

Long jump

		metres
1896	E.H. Clark (USA)	6.35
1900	A.C. Kraenzlein (USA)	7.18
1904	M. Prinstein (USA)	7.34
1908	F.C. Irons (USA)	7.48
1912	A.L. Gutterson (USA)	7.60
1920	W. Pettersson (Swe.)	7.15
1924	W. De H. Hubbard (USA)	7.44
1928	E.B. Hamm (USA)	7.73
1932	E.L. Gordon (USA)	7.64
1936	J.C. Owens (USA)	8.06
1948	W.S. Steele (USA)	7.82

1952	J.C. Biffle (USA)	7.57
1956	G.C. Bell (USA)	7.83
1960	R.H. Boston (USA)	8.12
1964	L. Davies (GB)	8.07
1968	R. Beamon (USA)	8.90
1972	R. Williams (USA)	8.24
1976	A. Robinson (USA)	8.35
1980	L. Dombrowski (GDR)	8.54

Triple jump

		metres
1896	J.V. Connolly (USA)	13.71
1900	M. Prinstein (USA)	14.47
1904	M. Prinstein (USA)	14.35
1908	T.J. Ahearne (GB/Ire.)	14.91
1912	G. Lindblom (Swe.)	14.76
1920	V. Tuulos (Fin.)	14.50
1924	A.W. Winter (Aus.)	15.52
1928	M. Oda (Japan)	15.21
1932	C. Nambu (Japan)	15.72
1936	N. Tajima (Japan)	16.00
1948	A.P. Ahman (Swe.)	15.40
1952	A.F. da Silva (Bra.)	16.22
1956	A.F. da Silva (Bra.)	16.35
1960	J. Szmidt (Pol.)	16.81
1964	J. Szmidt (Pol.)	16.85
1968	V. Saneyev (USSR)	17.39
1972	V. Saneyev (USSR)	17.35
1976	V. Saneyev (USSR)	17.29
1980	J. Uudmae (USSR)	17.35

Shot put

		metres
1896	R.S. Garrett (USA)	11.22
1900	R. Sheldon (USA)	14.10
1904	R.W. Rose (USA)	14.80
1908	R.W. Rose (USA)	14.21
1912	P.J. McDonald (USA)	15.34
1920	V. Porhola (Fin.)	14.81
1924	C.L. Houser (USA)	14.99
1928	J. Kuck (USA)	15.87
1932	L.J. Sexton (USA)	16.00
1936	H. Woelke (Germany)	16.20
1948	W.M. Thompson (USA)	17.12
1952	W.P. O'Brien (USA)	17.41
1956	W.P. O'Brien (USA)	18.57
1960	W.H. Nieder (USA)	19.68
1964	D.C. Long (USA)	20.33
1968	J.R. Matson (USA)	20.54
1972	W. Komar (Pol.)	21.18
1976	U. Beyer (GDR)	21.05
1980	V. Kiselyev (USSR)	21.35

Discus

		metres
1896	R.S. Garrett (USA)	29.14
1900	R. Bauer (Hung.)	36.04
1904	M.J. Sheridan (USA)	39.28
1908	M.J. Sheridan (USA)	40.88
1912	A.R. Taipale (Fin.)	45.20
1920	E. Niklander (Fin.)	44.68
1924	C.L. Houser (USA)	46.14
1928	C.L. Houser (USA)	47.32
1932	J.F. Anderson (USA)	49.98
1936	K.K. Carpenter (USA)	50.48
1948	A. Consolini (Italy)	52.78
1952	S.G. Iness (USA)	55.02
1956	A.A. Oerter (USA)	56.36
1960	A.A. Oerter (USA)	59.18
1964	A.A. Oerter (USA)	61.00
1968	A.A. Oerter (USA)	64.78
1972	L. Danek (Czech.)	64.40
1976	M. Wilkins (USA)	67.50
1980	V. Rashchupkin (USSR)	66.64

Hammer

		metres
1900	J.J. Flanagan (USA)	49.72
1904	J.J. Flanagan (USA)	51.22
1908	J.J. Flanagan (USA)	51.92
1912	M.J. McGrath (USA)	54.72
1920	P.J. Ryan (USA)	52.86
1924	F.D. Tootell (USA)	53.28
1928	P. O'Callaghan (Ire.)	51.38
1932	P. O'Callaghan (Ire.)	53.92
1936	K. Hein (Gemany)	56.48
1948	I. Nemeth (Hung.)	56.06
1952	J. Csermak (Hung.)	60.34
1956	H.V. Connolly (USA)	63.18
1960	V. Rudenkov (USSR)	67.10
1964	R. Klim (USSR)	69.74
1968	G. Zsivotzky (Hung.)	73.36
1972	A. Bondarchuk (USSR)	75.50
1976	Y. Sedykh (USSR)	77.52
1980	Y. Sedykh (USSR)	81.80

Javelin

		metres
1908	E.V. Lemming (Swe.)	54.82
1912	E.V. Lemming (Swe.)	60.64
1920	J.J. Myyra (Fin.)	65.78
1924	J.J. Myyra (Fin.)	62.96
1928	E.H. Lundkvist (Swe.)	66.60
1932	M.H. Jarvinen (Fin.)	72.70
1936	G. Stock (Germany)	71.84
1948	K.T. Rautavaara (Fin.)	69.76
1952	C.C. Young (USA)	73.78
1956	E. Danielson (Norway)	85.70
1960	V. Tsibulenko (USSR)	84.64
1964	P.L. Nevala (Fin.)	82.66
1968	J. Lusis (USSR)	90.10

1972	K. Wolfermann (FRG)	90.48
1976	M. Nemeth (Hung.)	94.58
1980	D. Kula (USSR)	91.20

Decathlon points
1912	H. Wieslander (Swe.)	6161*
1920	H. Lovland (Norway)	5970
1924	H.M. Osborn (USA)	6668
1928	P.I. Yrjola (Fin.)	6774
1932	J.A.B. Bausch (USA)	6896
1936	G.E. Morris (USA)	7421
1948	R.B. Mathias (USA)	6825
1952	R.B. Mathias (USA)	7731
1956	M.G. Campbell (USA)	7708
1960	R.L. Johnson (USA)	8001
1964	W. Holdorf (Germany)	7887
1968	W. Toomey (USA)	8193
1972	N. Avilov (USSR)	8456
1976	B. Jenner (USA)	8617
1980	F.M. Thompson (GB)	8495

* The original winner with 6845 points, J. Thorpe (USA), was later disqualified but has recently been reinstated as equal 1st.

20 kilometres walk h. min. sec.
1956	L. Spirin (USSR)	1	31	27.4
1960	V. Golubnichiy (USSR)	1	34	07.2
1964	K.J. Matthews (GB)	1	29	34.0
1968	V. Golubnichiy (USSR)	1	33	58.4
1972	P. Frenkel (GDR)	1	26	42.4
1976	D. Bautista (Mexico)	1	24	40.6
1980	M. Damilano (Italy)	1	23	35.5

50 kilometres walk h. min. sec.
1932	T.W. Green (GB)	4	50	10.0
1936	H.H. Whitlock (GB)	4	30	41.4
1948	J.A. Ljunggren (Swe.)	4	41	52.0
1952	G. Dordoni (Italy)	4	28	07.8
1956	N.R. Read (N.Z.)	4	30	42.8
1960	D.J. Thompson (GB)	4	25	30.0
1964	A. Pamich (Italy)	4	11	12.4
1968	C. Hohne (GDR)	4	20	11.6
1972	B. Kannenberg (FRG)	3	56	11.6
1976	Not held			
1980	H. Gauder (GDR)	3	49	24.0

Women's events
100 metres sec.
1928	E. Robinson (USA)	12.2

1932	S. Walasiewicz (Pol.)	11.9
1936	H.H. Stephens (USA)	11.5
1948	F.E. Blankers-Koen (H.)	11.9
1952	M. Jackson (Aus.)	11.5
1956	B. Cuthbert (Aus.)	11.5
1960	W.G. Rudolph (USA)	11.0
1964	W. Tyus (USA)	11.4
1968	W. Tyus (USA)	11.08
1972	R. Stecher (GDR)	11.07
1976	A. Richter (FRG)	11.08
1980	L. Kondratyeva (USSR)	11.06

200 metres sec.
1948	F.E. Blankers-Koen (H.)	24.4
1952	M. Jackson (Aus.)	23.7
1956	B. Cuthbertson (Aus.)	23.4
1960	W.G. Rudolph (USA)	24.0
1964	E.M. McGuire (USA)	23.0
1968	I. Szewinska (Pol.)	22.58
1972	R. Stecher (GDR)	22.40
1976	B. Wockel (GDR)	22.37
1980	B. Wockel (GDR)	22.03

400 metres sec.
1964	B. Cuthbert (Aus.)	52.0
1968	C. Besson (Fr.)	52.03
1972	M. Zehrt (GDR)	51.08
1976	I. Szewinska (Pol.)	49.29
1980	M. Koch (GDR)	48.88

800 metres min. sec.
1928	L. Radke (Germany)	2	16.8
1960	L. Shevtsova (USSR)	2	04.3
1964	A.E. Packer (GB)	2	01.1
1968	M. Manning (USA)	2	00.9
1972	H. Falck (FRG)	1	58.6
1976	T. Kazankina (USSR)	1	54.9
1980	N. Olizaryenko (USSR)	1	53.5

1500 metres min. sec.
1972	L. Bragina (USSR)	4	01.4
1976	T. Kazankina (USSR)	4	05.5
1980	T. Kazankina (USSR)	3	56.6

80 metres hurdles sec.
1932	M. Didrikson (USA)	11.7
1936	T. Valla (Italy)	11.7
1948	F.E. Blankers-Koen (H.)	11.2
1952	S.B. De La Hunty (Aus.)	10.9
1956	S.B. De La Hunty (Aus.)	10.7
1960	I. Press (USSR)	10.8
1964	K. Balzer (Germany)	10.5
1968	M. Caird (Aus.)	10.3

100 metres hurdles

		sec.
1972	A. Ehrhardt (GDR)	12.59
1976	J. Schaller (GDR)	12.77
1980	V. Komisova (USSR)	12.56

4 × 100 metres relay

		sec.
1928	Canada	48.4
1932	United States	47.0
1936	United States	46.9
1948	Netherlands	47.5
1952	United States	45.9
1956	Australia	44.5
1960	United States	44.5
1964	Poland	43.6
1968	United States	42.87
1972	West Germany	42.81
1976	East Germany	42.55
1980	East Germany	41.60

4 × 400 metres relay

		min. sec.
1972	East Germany	3 23.0
1976	East Germany	3 19.2
1980	USSR	3 20.2

High jump

		metres
1928	E. Catherwood (Canada)	1.59
1932	J. H. Shiley (USA)	1.65
1936	I. Csak (Hung.)	1.60
1948	A. Coachman (USA)	1.68
1952	E. C. Brand (S. Afr.)	1.67
1956	M. I. McDaniel (USA)	1.76
1960	I. Balas (Romania)	1.85
1964	I. Balas (Romania)	1.90
1968	M. Rezkova (Czech.)	1.82
1972	U. Meyfarth (FRG)	1.92
1976	R. Ackermann (GDR)	1.93
1980	S. Simeoni (Italy)	1.97

Long jump

		metres
1948	V. O. Gyarmati (Hung.)	5.69
1952	Y. W. Williams (N.Z.)	6.24
1956	E. Krzesinka (Pol.)	6.35
1960	V. Krepkina (USSR)	6.37
1964	M. D. Rand (GB)	6.76
1968	V. Viscopoleanu (Rom.)	6.82
1972	H. Rosendahl (FRG)	6.78
1976	A. Voigt (GDR)	6.72
1980	T. Kolpakova (USSR)	7.06

Shot

		metres
1948	M. O. M. Ostermeyer (Fr.)	13.75
1952	G. I. Zybina (USSR)	15.28
1956	T. A. Tyshkevich (USSR)	16.59

1960	T. Press (USSR)	17.32
1964	T. Press (USSR)	18.14
1968	M. Gummel (GDR)	19.61
1972	N. Chizhova (USSR)	21.03
1976	I. Khristova (Bul.)	21.16
1980	I. Slupianek (GDR)	22.41

Discus

		metres
1928	H. Konopacka (Pol.)	39.62
1932	L. Copeland (USA)	40.58
1936	G. Mauermayer (Ger.)	47.62
1948	M. O. M. Ostermeyer (Fr.)	41.92
1952	N. Romashkova (USSR)	51.42
1956	O. Fikotova (Czech.)	53.68
1960	N. Ponomaryeva (USSR)*	55.10
1964	T. Press (USSR)	57.26
1968	L. Manoliu (Romania)	58.28
1972	F. Melnik (USSR)	66.62
1976	E. Jahl (GDR)	69.00
1980	E. Jahl (GDR)	69.96

*née Romashkova

Javelin

		metres
1932	M. Didrikson (USA)	43.68
1936	T. Fleischer (Germany)	45.18
1948	H. Bauma (Austria)	45.56
1952	D. Zatopkova (Czech,)	50.46
1956	I. Jaunzeme (USSR)	53.86
1960	E. Ozolina (USSR)	55.98
1964	M. Penes (Romania)	60.54
1968	A. Nemeth (Hung.)	60.36
1972	R. Fuchs (GDR)	63.88
1976	R. Fuchs (GDR)	65.94
1980	M. Colon (Cuba)	68.40

Pentathlon

		points
1964	I. Press (USSR)	5246
1968	I. Mickler (FRG)	5098
1972	M. E. Peters (GB)	4801
1976	S. Siegl (GDR)	4745
1980	N. Tkachenko (USSR)	5083

European Championships
Gold medallists
Men's events

100 metres

		sec.
1934	C. D. Berger (Neth.)	10.6
1938	M. B. Osendarp (Neth.)	10.5
1946	J. Archer (GB)	10.6
1950	E. Bally (Fr.)	10.7
1954	H. Futterer (Germany)	10.5
1958	A. Hary (Germany)	10.3
1962	C. Piquemal (Fr.)	10.4

1966	W. J. Maniak (Pol.)	10.5
1969	V. Borzov (USSR)	10.4
1971	V. Borzov (USSR)	10.26
1974	V. Borzov (USSR)	10.27
1978	P. Mennea (Italy)	10.27
1982	F. Emmelmann (GDR)	10.21

200 metres

		sec.
1934	C. D. Berger (Neth.)	21.5
1938	M. B. Osendarp (Neth.)	21.2
1946	N. Karakulov (USSR)	21.6
1950	B. Shenton (GB)	21.5
1954	H. Futterer (Germany)	20.9
1958	M. Germar (Germany)	21.0
1962	O. Jonsson (Swe.)	20.7
1966	R. Bambuck (Fr.)	20.9
1969	P. Clerc (Switzerland)	20.6
1971	V. Borzov (USSR)	20.30
1974	P. Mennea (Italy)	20.60
1978	P. Mennea (Italy)	20.16
1982	O. Prenzler (GDR)	20.46

400 metres

		sec.
1934	A. Metzner (Germany)	47.9
1938	A. G. K. Brown (GB)	47.4
1946	N. Holst Sorensen (Den.)	47.9
1950	D. C. Pugh (GB)	47.3
1954	A. Ignatyev (USSR)	46.6
1958	J. D. Wrighton (GB)	46.3
1962	R. J. Brightwell (GB)	45.9
1966	S. Gredzinski (Pol.)	46.0
1968	J. Werner (Pol.)	45.7
1971	D. A. Jenkins (GB)	45.45
1974	K. Honz (FRG)	45.04
1978	F-P. Hofmeister (FRG)	45.73
1982	H. Weber (FRG)	44.72

800 metres

		min. sec.
1934	M. Szabo (Hung.)	1 52.0
1938	R. Harbig (Germany)	1 50.6
1946	R. Gustafsson (Swe.)	1 51.0
1950	H. J. Parlett (GB)	1 50.5
1954	L. Szentgali (Hung.)	1 47.1
1958	M. A. Rawson (GB)	1 47.8
1962	M. Matuschewski (Ger.)	1 50.5
1966	M. Matuschewski (Ger.)	1 45.9
1969	D. Fromm (GDR)	1 45.9
1971	Y. Arzhanov (USSR)	1 45.6
1974	L. Susanj (Yug.)	1 44.1
1978	O. Beyer (GDR)	1 43.8
1982	H-P. Ferner (FRG)	1 46.4

1500 metres

		min. sec.
1934	L. Beccali (Italy)	3 54.6

1938	S. C. Wooderson (GB)	3 53.6
1946	L. Strand (Swe.)	3 48.0
1950	W. F. Slijkhuis (Neth.)	3 47.2
1954	R. G. Bannister (GB)	3 43.8
1958	B. S. Hewson (GB)	3 41.9
1962	M. Jazy (Fr.)	3 40.9
1966	B. Tummler (FRG)	3 41.9
1969	J. H. Whetton (GB)	3 39.4
1971	F. Arese (Italy)	3 38.4
1974	K. P. Justus (GDR)	3 40.6
1978	S.M.J. Ovett (GB)	3 35.6
1982	S. Cram (GB)	3 36.5

5000 metres

		min. sec.
1934	R. Rochard (Fr.)	14 36.8
1938	T.A. Maki (Fin.)	14 26.8
1946	S.C. Wooderson (GB)	14 08.6
1950	E. Zatopek (Czech.)	14 03.0
1954	V. Kuts (USSR)	13 56.6
1958	Z. Krzyskowiak (Pol.)	13 53.4
1962	M.B.S. Tulloh (GB)	14 00.6
1966	M. Jazy (Fr.)	13 42.8
1969	I. Stewart (GB)	13 44.8
1971	J. Vaatainen (Fin.)	13 32.6
1974	B. Foster (GB)	13 17.2
1978	V. Ortis (Italy)	13 28.5
1982	T. Wessinghage (FRG)	13 28.9

10,000 metres

		min. sec.
1934	I. Salminen (Fin.)	31 02.6
1938	I. Salminen (Fin.)	30 52.4
1946	V. J. Heino (Fin.)	29 52.0
1950	E. Zatopek (Czech.)	29 12.0
1954	E. Zatopek (Czech.)	28 58.0
1958	Z. Krzyszkowiak (Pol.)	28 56.0
1962	P. Bolotnikov (USSR)	28 54.0
1966	J. Haase (GDR)	28 26.0
1969	J. Haase (GDR)	28 41.6
1971	J. Vaatainen (Fin.)	27 52.8
1974	M. Kuschmann (GDR)	28 25.8
1978	M. Vainio (Fin.)	27 31.0
1982	A. Cova (Italy)	27 41.1

Marathon

		h. min. sec.
1934	A.A. Toivonen (Fin.)	2 52 29.0
1938	V. Muinonen (Fin.)	2 37 28.8
1946	M. Hietanen (Fin.)	2 24 55.0
1950	J.T. Holden (GB)	2 32 13.2
1954	V.L. Karvonen (Fin.)	2 24 51.6
1958	S. Popov (USSR)	2 15 17.0
1962	B.L. Kilby (GB)	2 23 18.8
1966	J.J. Hogan (GB)	2 20 04.6
1969	R. Hill (GB)	2 16 47.8

1971	K. Lismont (Belg.)	2	13 09.0
1974	I.R. Thompson (GB)	2	13 18.8
1978	L. Moseyev (USSR)	2	11 57.5
1982	G. Nijboer (Neth.)	2	15 16.0

3000 metres steeplechase

		min. sec.
1938	L.A. Larsson (Swe.)	9 16.2
1946	R. Pujazon (Fr.)	9 01.4
1950	J. Roudny (Czech.)	9 05.4
1954	S. Rozsnyoi (Hung.)	8 49.6
1958	J. Chromik (Pol.)	8 38.2
1962	G. Roelants (Belg.)	8 32.6
1966	V. Kudinskiy (USSR)	8 26.6
1969	M. Zhelev (Bulg.)	8 25.0
1971	J-P. Villain (Fr.)	8 25.2
1974	B. Malinowski (Pol.)	8 15.0
1978	B. Malinowski (Pol.)	8 15.1
1982	P. Ilg (FRG)	8 18.6

110 metres hurdles

		sec.
1934	J. Kovacs (Hung.)	14.8
1938	D.O. Finlay (GB)	14.3
1946	E.H. Lidman (Swe.)	14.6
1950	A.J. Marie (Fr.)	14.6
1954	Y. Bulanchik (USSR)	14.4
1958	K.M. Lauer (Germany)	13.7
1962	A. Mikailov (USSR)	13.8
1966	E. Ottoz (Italy)	13.7
1969	E. Ottoz (Italy)	13.5
1971	F. Siebeck (GDR)	14.00
1974	G. Drut (Fr.)	13.40
1978	T. Munkelt (GDR)	13.54
1982	T. Munkelt (GDR)	13.41

400 metres hurdles

		sec.
1934	H. Scheele (Germany)	53.2
1938	P. Joye (Fr.)	53.1
1946	B. Storskrubb (Fin.)	52.2
1950	A. Filiput (Italy)	51.9
1954	A. Yulin (USSR)	50.5
1958	Y. Lituyev (USSR)	51.1
1962	S. Morale (Italy)	49.2
1966	R. Frinolli (Italy)	49.8
1969	V. Skomorokhov (USSR)	49.7
1971	J-C Nallet (Fr.)	49.2
1974	A.P. Pascoe (GB)	48.82
1978	H. Schmid (FRG)	48.51
1982	H. Schmid (FRG)	47.48

4 × 100 metres relay

		sec.
1934	Germany	41.0
1938	Germany	40.9
1946	Sweden	41.5

1950	Russia	41.5
1954	Hungary	40.6
1958	Germany	40.2
1962	Germany	39.5
1966	France	39.4
1969	France	38.8
1971	Czechoslovakia	39.3
1974	France	38.69
1978	Poland	38.58
1982	USSR	38.60

4 × 400 metres relay

		min. sec.
1934	Germany	3 14.1
1938	Germany	3 13.7
1946	France	3 14.4
1950	Great Britain	3 10.2
1954	France	3 08.7
1958	Great Britain	3 07.9
1962	Germany	3 05.8
1966	Poland	3 04.5
1969	France	3 02.3
1971	West Germany	3 02.9
1974	Great Britain	3 03.3
1978	West Germany	3 02.0
1982	West Germany	3 00.6

High jump

		metres
1934	K. Kotkas (Fin.)	2.00
1938	K. Lundqvist (Swe.)	1.97
1946	A. Bolinder (Swe.)	1.99
1950	A.S. Paterson (GB)	1.96
1954	B. Nilsson (Swe.)	2.02
1958	R. Dahl (Swe.)	2.12
1962	V. Brumel (USSR)	2.21
1966	J. Madubost (Fr.)	2.12
1969	V. Gavrilov (USSR)	2.17
1971	K. Sapka (USSR)	2.20
1974	J. Torring (Denmark)	2.25
1978	V. Yashchenko (USSR)	2.30
1982	D. Mogenburg (FRG)	2.30

Pole vault

		metres
1934	G. Wegner (Germany)	4.00
1938	K. Sutter (Germany)	4.05
1946	A. Lindberg (Swe.)	4.17
1950	R.L. Lundberg (Swe.)	4.30
1954	E. Landstrom (Fin.)	4.30
1958	E. Landstrom (Fin.)	4.50
1962	P. Nikula (Fin.)	4.80
1966	W. Nordwig (GDR)	5.10
1969	W. Nordwig (GDR)	5.30
1971	W. Nordwig (GDR)	5.35
1974	V. Kishkun (USSR)	5.35

1978	V. Trofimenko (USSR)	5.55
1982	A. Krupsky (USSR)	5.60

Long jump
metres

1934	W. Leichum (Germany)	7.45
1938	W. Leichum (Germany)	7.65
1946	O. Laessker (Swe.)	7.42
1950	T. Bryngeirsson (Ice.)	7.32
1954	O. Foldessy (Hung.)	7.51
1958	I. Ter-Ovanesyan (USSR)	7.81
1962	I. Ter-Ovanesyan (USSR)	8.19
1966	L. Davies (GB)	7.98
1969	I. Ter-Ovanesyan (USSR)	8.17
1971	M. Klauss (GDR)	7.92
1974	V. Podluzny (USSR)	8.12
1978	J. Rousseau (Fr.)	8.18
1982	L. Dombrowski (GDR)	8.41

Triple jump
metres

1934	W. Peters (Neth.)	14.89
1938	O. Rajasaari (Fin.)	15.32
1946	K.J.V. Rautio (Fin.)	15.17
1950	L. Shcherbakov (USSR)	15.39
1954	L. Shcherbakov (USSR)	15.90
1958	J. Szmidt (Pol.)	16.43
1962	J. Szmidt (Pol.)	16.55
1966	G. Stoikovski (Bulg.)	16.67
1969	V. Saneyev (USSR)	17.34
1971	J. Drehmel (GDR)	17.16
1974	V. Saneyev (USSR)	17.23
1978	M. Srejovic (Yug.)	16.94
1982	K. Connor (GB)	17.29

Shot
metres

1934	A. Viiding (Estonia)	15.19
1938	A. Kreek (Estonia)	15.83
1946	G. Huseby (Iceland)	15.56
1950	G. Huseby (Iceland)	16.74
1954	J. Skobla (Czech.)	17.20
1958	A. Rowe (GB)	17.78
1962	V. Varju (Hung.)	19.02
1966	V. Varju (Hung.)	19.43
1969	D. Hoffman (GDR)	20.12
1971	H. Briesnick (GDR)	21.08
1974	H. Briesnick (GDR)	20.50
1978	U. Beyer (GDR)	21.08
1982	U. Beyer (GDR)	21.50

Discus
metres

1934	H. Anderson (Swe.)	50.38
1938	W. Schroeder (Germany)	49.70
1946	A. Consolini (Italy)	53.22
1950	A. Consolini (Italy)	53.74

1954	A. Consolini (Italy)	53.44
1958	E. Piatkowski (Pol.)	53.92
1962	V. Trusenyov (USSR)	57.10
1966	D. Thorith (GDR)	57.42
1969	H. Losch (GDR)	61.82
1971	L. Danek (Czech.)	63.90
1974	P. Kahma (Fin.)	63.62
1978	R. Schmidt (GDR)	66.82
1982	I. Bugar (Czech.)	66.64

Hammer
metres

1934	V. Porhola (Fin.)	50.34
1938	K. Hein (Germany)	58.76
1946	B. Ericson (Swe.)	56.44
1950	S. Strandli (Norway)	55.70
1954	M. Krivonosov (USSR)	63.34
1958	T. Rut (Pol.)	64.78
1962	G. Zsivotzky (Hung.)	69.64
1966	R. Klim (USSR)	70.02
1969	A. Bondarchuk (USSR)	74.68
1971	W. Beyer (FRG)	72.36
1974	A. Spiridonov (USSR)	74.20
1978	Y. Sedykh (USSR)	77.28
1982	Y. Sedykh (USSR)	81.66

Javelin
metres

1934	M.H. Jarvinen (Fin.)	76.66
1938	M.H. Jarvinen (Fin.)	76.86
1946	A.L.F. Atterwall (Swe.)	68.74
1950	T. Hyytiainen (Fin.)	71.26
1954	J. Sidlo (Pol.)	76.34
1958	J. Sidlo (Pol.)	80.18
1962	J. Lusis (USSR)	82.04
1966	J. Lusis (USSR)	84.48
1969	J. Lusis (USSR)	91.52
1971	J. Lusis (USSR)	90.68
1974	H. Siitonen (Fin.)	89.58
1978	M. Wessing (FRG)	89.12
1982	U. Hohn (GDR)	91.34

Decathlon
points

1934	H.H. Sievert (Germany)	6858
1938	O. Bexell (Swe.)	6870
1946	G. Holmvang (Norway)	6760
1950	I. Heinrich (France)	7009
1954	V. Kuznyetsov (USSR)	7043
1958	V. Kuznyetsov (USSR)	7697
1962	V. Kuznyetsov (USSR)	7770
1966	W. von Moltke (FRG)	7740
1969	J. Kirst (GDR)	8041
1971	J. Kirst (GDR)	8196
1974	R. Skowronek (Pol.)	8207
1978	A. Grebenyuk (USSR)	8340
1982	F. M. Thompson (GB)	8743

10,000 metres walk

		min. sec.
1946	J.F. Mikaelsson (Swe.)	46 05.2
1950	F. Schwab (Switz.)	46 01.8
1954	J. Dolezal (Czech.)	45 01.8

20 kilometres walk

		h. min. sec.
1958	S.F. Vickers (GB)	1 33 09.0
1962	K.J. Matthews (GB)	1 35 54.8
1966	D. Lindner (GDR)	1 29 25.0
1969	V.P. Nihill (GB)	1 30 41.0
1971	N. Smaga (USSR)	1 27 20.2
1974	V. Golubnichiy (USSR)	
		1 29 30.3
1978	R. Wieser (GDR)	1 23 11.5
1982	J. Marin (Spain)	1 23 43.0

50 kilometres walk

		h. min. sec.
1934	J. Dalins (Latvia)	4 49 52.6
1938	H.H. Whitlock (GB)	4 41 51.0
1946	J. Ljunggren (Swe.)	4 38 20.0
1950	G. Dordoni (Italy)	4 40 42.6
1954	V. Ukhov (USSR)	4 22 11.2
1958	Y. Maskinskov (USSR)	
		4 17 15.4
1962	A. Pamich (Italy)	4 18 46.6
1966	A. Pamich (Italy)	4 18 42.2
1969	C. Hohne (GDR)	4 13 32.8
1971	V. Soldatenko (USSR)	
		4 02 22.0
1974	C. Hohne (GDR)	3 59 05.6
1978	J. Llopart (Spain)	3 53 29.9
1982	R. Salonen (Fin.)	3 55 29.0

Women's events

100 metres

		sec.
1938	S. Walasiewicz (Pol.)	11.9
1946	Y. Sechenova (USSR)	11.9
1950	F.E. Blankers-Koen (Neth.)	11.7
1954	I. Turova (USSR)	11.8
1958	H.J. Young (GB)	11.7
1962	D. Hyman (GB)	11.3
1966	E. Klobukowska (Pol.)	11.5
1969	P. Vogt (GDR)	11.6
1971	R. Stecher (GDR)	11.35
1974	I. Szewinska (Pol.)	11.13
1978	M. Gohr (GDR)	11.13
1982	M. Gohr (GDR)	11.01

200 metres

		sec.
1938	S. Walasiewicz (Pol.)	23.8
1946	Y. Sechenova (USSR)	25.4

1950	F.E. Blankers-Koen (Neth.)	24.0
1954	M. Itkina (USSR)	24.3
1958	B. Janiszewska (Pol.)	24.1
1962	J. Heine (Germany)	23.5
1966	I. Szewinska (Pol.)	23.1
1969	P. Vogt (GDR)	23.2
1971	R. Stecher (GDR)	22.71
1974	I. Szewinska (Pol.)	22.51
1978	L. Kondratyeva (USSR)	22.52
1982	B. Wockel (GDR)	22.04

400 metres

		sec.
1958	M. Itkina (USSR)	53.7
1962	M. Itkina (USSR)	53.4
1966	A. Chmelkova (Czech.)	52.9
1969	N. Duclos (Fr.)	51.72
1971	H. Seidler (GDR)	52.1
1974	M. Salin (Fin.)	50.14
1978	M. Koch (GDR)	48.94
1982	M. Koch (GDR)	48.15

800 metres

		min. sec.
1954	N. Otkalenko (USSR)	2 08.8
1958	Y. Yermolayeva (USSR)	2 06.3
1962	G. Kraan (Neth.)	2 02.8
1966	V. Nikolic (Yug.)	2 02.8
1969	L. B. Board (GB)	2 01.4
1971	V. Nikolic (Yug.)	2 00.0
1974	L. Tomova (Bulg.)	1 58.1
1978	T. Providokhina (USSR)	1 55.8
1982	O. Mineyeva (USSR)	1 55.5

1500 metres

		min. sec.
1969	J. Jehlickova (Czech.)	4 10.7
1971	K. Burneleit (GDR)	4 09.6
1974	G. Hoffmeister (GDR)	4 02.3
1978	G. Romanova (USSR)	3 59.0
1982	O. Dvirna (USSR)	3 57.9

3000 metres

		min. sec.
1974	N. Holmen (Fin.)	8 55.2
1978	S. Ulmasova (USSR)	8 33.2
1982	S. Ulmasova (USSR)	8 30.3

80 metres hurdles

		sec.
1938	C. Testoni (Italy)	11.6
1946	F.E. Blankers-Koen (Neth.)	11.8
1950	F.E. Blankers-Koen (Neth.)	11.1
1954	M. Golubnichaya (USSR)	11.0
1958	G. Bystrova (USSR)	10.9
1962	T. Ciepla (Pol.)	10.6
1966	K. Balzer (GDR)	10.7

100 metres hurdles

		sec.
1969	K. Balzer (GDR)	13.3
1971	K. Balzer (GDR)	12.94
1974	A. Ehrhardt (GDR)	12.66
1978	J. Klier (GDR)	12.62
1982	L. Kalek (Pol.)	12.45

400 metres hurdles

		sec.
1978	T. Zelentsova (USSR)	54.89
1982	A-L. Skoglund (Swe.)	54.58

4 × 100 metres relay

		sec.
1938	Germany	46.8
1946	Netherlands	47.8
1950	Great Britain	47.4
1954	USSR	45.8
1958	USSR	45.3
1962	Poland	44.5
1966	Poland	44.4
1969	East Germany	43.6
1971	West Germany	43.3
1974	East Germany	42.51
1978	USSR	42.54
1982	East Germany	42.19

4 × 400 metres relay

		min. sec.
1969	Great Britain	3 30.8
1971	East Germany	3 29.3
1974	East Germany	3 25.2
1978	East Germany	3 21.2
1982	East Germany	3 19.1

High jump

		metres
1938	I. Csak (Hung.)	1.64
1946	A. Colchen (Fr.)	1.60
1950	S. Alexander (GB)	1.63
1954	T. E. Hopkins (GB)	1.67
1958	I. Balas (Romania)	1.77
1962	I. Balas (Romania)	1.83
1966	T. Chenchik (USSR)	1.75
1969	M. Rezkova (Czech.)	1.83
1971	I. Gusenbauer (Austria)	1.87
1974	R. Witschas (GDR)	1.95
1978	S. Simeoni (Italy)	2.01
1982	U. Meyfarth (FRG)	2.02

Long jump

		metres
1938	I. Praetz (Germany)	5.88
1946	G.J.M. Koudijs (Neth.)	5.67
1950	V. Bogdanova (USSR)	5.82
1954	J.C. Desforges (GB)	6.04
1958	L. Jacobi (Germany)	6.14
1962	T. Shchelkanova (USSR)	6.36

1966	I. Szewinska (Pol.)	6.55
1969	M. Sarna (Pol.)	6.49
1971	I. Mickler (FRG)	6.76
1974	I. Bruzsenyak (Hung.)	6.65
1978	V. Bardauskiene (USSR)	6.88
1982	V. Ionescu (Romania)	6.79

Shot

		metres
1938	H. Schroder (Germany)	13.29
1946	T. Sevryukova (USSR)	14.16
1950	A. Andreyeva (USSR)	14.32
1954	G. Zybina (USSR)	15.65
1958	M. Werner (Germany)	15.74
1962	T. Press (USSR)	18.55
1966	N. Chizhova (USSR)	17.22
1969	N. Chizhova (USSR)	20.43
1971	N. Chizhova (USSR)	20.16
1974	N. Chizhova (USSR)	20.78
1978	I. Slupianek (GDR)	21.41
1982	I. Slupianek (GDR)	21.59

Discus

		metres
1938	G. Mauermayer (Ger.)	44.80
1946	N. Dumbadze (USSR)	44.52
1950	N. Dumbadze (USSR)	48.02
1954	N. Ponomaryeva (USSR)	48.02
1958	T. Press (USSR)	52.32
1962	T. Press (USSR)	56.90
1966	C. Spielberg (GDR)	57.76
1969	T. Danilova (USSR)	59.28
1971	F. Melnik (USSR)	64.22
1974	F. Melnik (USSR)	69.00
1978	E. Jahl (GDR)	66.98
1982	T. Hristova (Bulg.)	68.34

Javelin

		metres
1938	L. Gelius (Germany)	45.58
1946	K. Mayuchaya (USSR)	46.24
1950	N. Smirnitskaya (USSR)	47.54
1954	D. Zatopkova (Czech.)	52.90
1958	D. Zatopkova (Czech.)	56.02
1962	E. Ozolina	54.92
1966	M. Luttge (GDR)	58.74
1969	A. Ranky (Hung.)	59.76
1971	D. Jaworska (Pol.)	61.00
1974	R. Fuchs (GDR)	67.22
1978	R. Fuchs (GDR)	69.16
1982	A. Verouli (Greece)	70.02

Pentathlon

		points
1950	A. Ben Hamo (Fr.)	3544
1954	A. Chudina (USSR)	4020
1958	G. Bystrova (USSR)	4215

1962 G. Bystrova (USSR)	4312	1938 W. Roberts (Eng.)	47.9
1966 V. Tikhomirova (USSR)	4272	1950 E.W. Carr (Aus.)	47.9
1969 L. Prokop (Austria)	4419	1954 R.K. Gosper (Aus.)	47.2
1971 H. Rosendahl (FRG)	4675	1958 Milkha Singh (India)	46.6
1974 N. Tkachenko (USSR)	4776	1962 G.E. Kerr (Jam.)	46.7
1978 M. Papp (Hung.)	4655	1966 W. Mottley (Tri.)	45.0

Heptathlon points
1982 R. Neubert (GDR) 6622

400 metres	sec.
1970 C. Asati (Kenya)	45.0
1974 C. Asati (Kenya)	46.04
1978 R. Mitchell (Aus.)	46.34
1982 B. Cameron (Jam.)	45.89

British Empire and Commonwealth Games Track and field gold medallists
Men's events

100 yards	sec.
1930 P. Williams (Canada)	9.9
1934 A.W. Sweeney (Eng.)	10.0
1938 C.B. Holmes (Eng.)	9.7
1950 J.F. Treloar (Aus.)	9.7
1954 M.G.R. Agostini (Tri.)	9.6
1958 K.A.St.H. Gardner (Jam.)	9.4
1962 S. Antao (Kenya)	9.5
1966 H.W. Jerome (Canada)	9.4

100 metres	sec.
1970 D. Quarrie (Jam.)	10.2
1974 D. Quarrie (Jam.)	10.38
1978 D. Quarrie (Jam.)	10.03
1982 A. Wells (Scot.)	10.02

200 yards	sec.
1930 S.E. Englehart (Eng.)	21.8
1934 A.W. Sweeney (Eng.)	21.9
1938 C.B. Holmes (Eng.)	21.2
1950 J.F. Treloar (Aus.)	21.5
1954 D.W. Jowett (N.Z.)	21.5
1958 T.A. Robinson (Bah.)	21.0
1962 S. Antao (Kenya)	21.1
1966 S.F. Allotey (Ghana)	20.7

200 metres	sec.
1970 D. Quarrie (Jam.)	20.5
1974 D. Quarrie (Jam.)	20.73
1978 A. Wells (Scot.)	20.12
1982 M. McFarlane (Eng.) and A. Wells (Scot.)	20.43

440 yards	sec.
1930 A. Wilson (Canada)	48.8
1934 G.L. Rampling (Eng.)	48.0

880 yards	min. sec.
1930 T. Hampson (Eng.)	1 52.4
1934 P.A. Edwards (B. Guiana)	1 54.2
1938 V.P. Boot (N.Z.)	1 51.2
1950 H.J. Parlett (Eng.)	1 53.1
1954 D.J.N. Johnson (Eng.)	1 50.7
1958 H.J. Elliott (Aus.)	1 49.3
1962 P.G. Snell (N.Z.)	1 47.6
1966 N.S. Clough (Aus.)	1 46.9

800 metres	min. sec.
1970 R. Ouko (Kenya)	1 46.8
1974 J. Kipkurgat (Kenya)	1 43.9
1978 M. Boit (Kenya)	1 46.4
1982 P. Bourke (Aus.)	1 45.2

Mile	min. sec.
1930 R.H. Thomas (Eng.)	4 14.0
1934 J.E. Lovelock (N.Z.)	4 12.8
1938 J.W.Ll. Alford (Wales)	4 11.6
1950 C.W. Parnell (Canada)	4 11.0
1954 R.G. Bannister (Eng.)	3 58.8
1958 H.J. Elliott (Aus.)	3 59.0
1962 P.G. Snell (N.Z.)	4 04.6
1966 K. Keino (Kenya)	3 55.3

1500 metres	min. sec.
1970 K. Keino (Kenya)	3 36.6
1974 F. Bayi (Tanzania)	3 32.2
1978 D.R. Moorcroft (Eng.)	3 35.5
1982 S. Cram (Eng.)	3 42.4

3 miles	min. sec.
1930 S.A. Tomlin (Eng.)	14 27.4
1934 W.J. Beavers (Eng.)	14 32.6
1938 C.H. Matthews (N.Z.)	13 59.6
1950 L. Eyre (Eng.)	14 23.6
1954 C.J. Chataway (Eng.)	13 35.2
1958 M.G. Halberg (N.Z.)	13 15.0
1962 M.G. Halberg (N.Z.)	13 34.2

1966 K. Keino (Kenya)   12 57.4

5000 metres   min. sec.
1970 I. Stewart (Scot.)   13 22.8
1974 B. Jipcho (Kenya)   13 14.0
1978 H. Rono (Kenya)   13 23.0
1982 D. Moorcroft (Eng.)   13 33.0

6 miles   min. sec.
1930 W.J. Savidan (N.Z.)   30 49.6
1934 A.W. Penny (Eng.)   31 00.6
1938 C.H. Matthews (N.Z.)   30 14.5
1950 W.H. Nelson (N.Z.)   30 29.6
1954 P.B. Driver (Eng.)   29 09.4
1958 W.D. Power (Aus.)   28 47.8
1962 B. Kidd (Canada)   28 26.6
1966 N. Temu (Kenya)   27 14.6

10,000 metres   min. sec.
1970 J.L. Stewart (Scot.)   28 11.8
1974 R. Tayler (N.Z.)   27 46.4
1978 B. Foster (Eng.)   28 13.7
1982 G. Shahanga (Tanzania) 28 10.6

Marathon   h. min. sec.
1930 D.McL. Wright (Scot.)
                      2 43 43.0
1934 H. Webster (Canada) 2 40 36.0
1938 J.L. Coleman (S.A.)   2 30 49.8
1950 J.T. Holden (Eng.)   2 32 57.0
1954 J. McGhee (Scot.)   2 39 36.0
1958 W.D. Power (Aus.)   2 22 45.6
1962 B.L. Kilby (Eng.)   2 21 17.0
1966 J.N.C. Alder (Scot.)   2 22 07.8
1970 R. Hill (Eng.)   2 09 28.0
1974 I.R. Thompson (Eng.) 2 09 12.0
1978 G. Shahanga (Tan.)   2 15 39.8
1982 R. De Castella (Aus.) 2 09 18.0

Steeplechase   min. sec.
1930 G.W. Bailey (Eng.)   9 52.0
1934 S.C. Scarsbrook (Eng.) 10 23.4

3000 metres steeplechase   min. sec.
1962 T.A. Vincent (Aus.)   8 43.4
1966 R.P. Welsh (N.Z.)   8 29.6
1970 A.P. Manning (Aus.)   8 26.2
1974 B. Jipcho (Kenya)   8 20.8
1978 H. Rono (Kenya)   8 26.5
1982 J. Korir (Kenya)   8 24.0

120 yards hurdles   sec.
1930 Lord Burghley (Eng.)   14.6

1934 D.O. Finlay (Eng.)   15.2
1938 T.P. Lavery (S.A.)   14.0
1950 P.J. Gardner (Aus.)   14.3
1954 K.A.St.H. Gardner (Jam.) 14.2
1958 K.A.St.H. Gardner (Jam.) 14.0
1962 H.G. Raziq (Pakistan)   14.3
1966 D.P. Hemery (Eng.)   14.1

110 metres hurdles   sec.
1970 D.P. Hemery (Eng.)   13.6
1974 F. Kimaiyo (Kenya)   13.69
1978 B. Price (Wales)   13.70
1982 M. McKoy (Canada)   13.37

440 yards hurdles   sec.
1930 Lord Burghley (Eng.)   54.4
1934 F.A.R. Hunter (Scot.)   55.2
1938 J.W. Loaring (Canada)   52.9
1950 D. White (Ceylon)   52.5
1954 D.F. Lean (Aus.)   52.4
1958 G.C. Potgeiter (S.A.)   49.7
1962 K.J. Roche (Aus.)   51.5
1966 K.J. Roche (Aus.)   51.0

400 metres hurdles   sec.
1970 J. Sherwood (Eng.)   50.0
1974 A.P. Pascoe (Eng.)   48.83
1978 D. Kimaiyo (Kenya)   49.48
1982 G. Brown (Aus.)   49.37

4 × 110 yards relay   sec.
1930 Canada   42.2
1934 England   42.2
1938 Canada   41.6
1950 Australia   42.2
1954 Canada   41.3
1958 England   40.7
1962 England   40.6
1966 Ghana   39.8

4 × 100 metres relay   sec.
1970 Jamaica   39.4
1974 Australia   39.3
1978 Scotland   39.24
1982 Nigeria   39.15

4 × 440 yards relay   min. sec.
1930 England   3 19.4
1934 England   3 16.8
1938 Canada   3 16.9
1950 Australia   3 17.8
1954 England   3 11.2
1958 South Africa   3 08.1

| 1962 | Jamaica | 3 | 10.2 |
| 1966 | Trinidad & Tobago | 3 | 02.8 |

4 × 400 metres relay   min. sec.

1970	Kenya	3	03.6
1974	Kenya	3	04.4
1978	Kenya	3	03.5
1982	England	3	05.5

High jump   metres

1930	J.H. Viljoen (S.A.)	1.90
1934	E.T. Thacker (S.A.)	1.90
1938	E.T. Thacker (S.A.)	1.95
1950	J.A. Winter (Aus.)	1.98
1954	E.A. Ifeajuna (Nig.)	2.03
1958	E. Haisley (Jam.)	2.05
1962	P.F. Hobson (Aus.)	2.11
1966	L. Peckham (Aus.)	2.08
1970	L. Peckham (Aus.)	2.14
1974	G. Windeyer (Aus.)	2.16
1978	C. Ferragne (Canada)	2.20
1982	M. Ottey (Canada)	2.31

Pole vault   metres

1930	V.W. Pickard (Canada)	3.73
1934	C.J.S. Apps (Canada)	3.81
1938	A.S. du Plessis (S.A.)	4.11
1950	T.D. Anderson (Eng.)	3.96
1954	G.M. Elliott (Eng.)	4.26
1958	G.M. Elliott (Eng.)	4.16
1962	T.S. Bickle (Aus.)	4.49
1966	T.S. Bickle (Aus.)	4.80
1970	M.A. Bull (N. Ire.)	5.10
1974	D. Baird (Aus.)	5.05
1978	B. Simpson (Canada)	5.10
1982	R. Boyd (Aus.)	5.20

Long jump   metres

1930	L. Hutton (Canada)	7.20
1934	S. Richardson (Canada)	7.17
1938	H. Brown (Canada)	7.43
1950	N.G. Price (S.A.)	7.31
1954	K.S.D. Wilmshurst (Eng.)	7.54
1958	P. Foreman (Jam.)	7.47
1962	M. Ahey (Ghana)	8.05
1966	L. Davies (Wales)	7.99
1970	L. Davies (Wales)	8.06
1974	A.L. Lerwill (Eng.)	7.94
1978	R.R. Mitchell (Eng.)	8.06
1982	G. Honey (Aus.)	8.13

Triple jump   metres

| 1930 | G.C. Smallacombe (Can.) | 14.76 |

1934	J.P. Metcalfe (Aus.)	15.63
1938	J.P. Metcalfe (Aus.)	15.49
1950	B.T. Oliver (Aus.)	15.61
1954	K.S.D. Wilmshurst (Eng.)	15.28
1958	I.R. Tomlinson (Aus.)	15.73
1962	I.R. Tomlinson (Aus.)	16.20
1966	S. Igun (Nigeria)	16.40
1970	P.J. May (Aus.)	16.72
1974	J. Owusu (Ghana)	16.50
1978	K.L. Connor (Eng.)	17.21
1982	K.L. Connor (Eng.)	17.81

Shot   metres

1930	H.B. Hart (S.A.)	14.58
1934	H.B. Hart (S.A.)	14.67
1938	L.A. Fouche (S.A.)	14.48
1950	M. Tuicakau (Fiji)	14.63
1954	J.A. Savidge (Eng.)	16.77
1958	A. Rowe (Eng.)	17.57
1962	M.T. Lucking (Eng.)	18.08
1966	D. Steen (Canada)	18.79
1970	D. Steen (Canada)	19.21
1974	G.L. Capes (Eng.)	20.74
1978	G.L. Capes (Eng.)	19.77
1982	B. Pauletto (Canada)	19.55

Discus   metres

1930	H.B. Hart (S.A.)	41.44
1934	H.B. Hart (S.A.)	41.54
1938	E.E. Coy (Canada)	44.76
1950	I.M. Reed (Aus.)	47.72
1954	S.J. du Plessis (S.A.)	51.70
1958	S.J. du Plessis (S.A.)	55.94
1962	W.P. Selvey (Aus.)	56.48
1966	L.R. Mills (N.Z.)	56.18
1970	G. Puce (Canada)	59.04
1974	R. Tait (N.Z.)	63.08
1978	B. Chambul (Canada)	59.70
1982	B. Cooper (Bahamas)	64.04

Hammer   metres

1930	M.C. Nokes (Eng.)	47.12
1934	M.C. Nokes (Eng.)	48.24
1938	G.W. Sutherland (Can.)	48.72
1950	D.McD.M. Clark (Scot.)	49.94
1954	M. Iqbal (Pakistan)	55.38
1958	M.J. Ellis (Eng.)	62.90
1962	A.H. Payne (Eng.)	61.64
1966	A.H. Payne (Eng.)	61.98
1970	A.H. Payne (Eng.)	67.80
1974	I.A. Chipchase (Eng.)	69.56
1978	P. Farmer (Aus.)	71.10
1982	R. Weir (Eng.)	75.08

Javelin	metres
1930 S.A. Lay (N.Z.)	63.12
1934 R. Dixon (Canada)	60.02
1938 J.A. Courtwright (Canada)	62.82
1950 L.J. Roininen (Canada)	57.10
1954 J.D. Achurch (Aus.)	68.52
1958 C.G. Smith (Eng.)	71.28
1962 A.E. Mitchell (Aus.)	78.10
1966 J.H.P. FitzSimmons (Eng.)	79.78
1970 D.H. Travis (Eng.)	79.50
1974 C.P. Clover (Eng.)	84.92
1978 P. Olsen (Canada)	84.00
1982 M. O'Rourke (N.Z.)	89.48

Decathlon	points
1966 R.A. Williams (N.Z.)	7270
1970 G.J. Smith (Aus.)	7492
1974 M.A. Bull (N. Ire.)	7417
1978 F.M. Thompson (Eng.)	8467
1982 F.M. Thompson (Eng.)	8410

20 mile walk	h. min. sec.
1966 R. Wallwork (Eng.)	2 44 42.8
1970 N.F. Freeman (Aus.)	2 33 33.0
1974 J. Warhurst (Eng.)	2 35 23.0

30 kilometres walk	h. min. sec.
1978 O.T. Flynn (Eng.)	2 22 03.7
1982 S. Barry (Wales)	2 10 16.0

Women's events

100 yards	sec.
1934 E.M. Hiscock (Eng.)	11.3
1938 D. Norman (Aus.)	11.1
1950 M. Jackson (Aus.)	10.8
1954 M. Nelson (Aus.)*	10.7
1958 M.J. Willard (Aus.)	10.6
1962 D. Hyman (Eng.)	11.2
1966 D. Burge (Aus.)	10.6

100 metres	sec.
1970 R.A. Boyle (Aus.)	11.2
1974 R.A. Boyle (Aus.)	11.27
1978 S.M. Lannaman (Eng.)	11.27
1982 A. Taylor (Canada)	11.00

220 yards	sec.
1934 E.M. Hiscock (Eng.)	25.0
1938 D. Norman (Aus.)	24.7
1950 M. Jackson (Aus.)	24.3
1954 M. Nelson (Aus.)*	24.0
1958 M.J. Willard (Aus.)	23.6

*née Jackson

1962 D. Hyman (Eng.)	23.8
1966 D. Burge (Aus.)	23.8

200 metres	sec.
1970 R.A. Boyle (Aus.)	22.7
1974 R.A. Boyle (Aus.)	22.50
1978 D. Boyd (Aus.)	22.82
1982 M. Ottey (Jam.)	22.19

440 yards	sec.
1966 J. Pollock (Aus.)	53.0

400 metres	sec.
1970 M. Neufville (Jam.)	51.0
1974 Y. Saunders (Canada)	51.67
1978 D-M.L. Hartley (Eng.)	51.69
1982 R. Boyle (Aus.)	51.26

880 yards	min. sec.
1934 G.A. Lunn (Eng.)	2 19.4
1962 D. Willis (Aus.)	2 03.7
1966 A. Hoffman (Canada)	2 04.3

800 metres	min. sec.
1970 R.O. Stirling (Scot.)	2 06.2
1974 C. Rendina (Aus.)	2 01.1
1978 J. Peckham (Aus.)	2 02.8
1982 K. McDermott (Wales)	2 01.4

1500 metres	min. sec.
1970 R. Ridley (Eng.)	4 18.8
1974 G. Reiser (Canada)	4 07.8
1978 M. Stewart (Eng.)	4 06.3
1982 C. Boxer (Eng.)	4 08.3

3000 metres	min. sec.
1978 P. Fudge (Eng.)	9 13.0
1982 A. Audain (N.Z.)	8 45.6

80 metres hurdles	sec.
1934 M.R. Clark (S.A.)	11.8
1938 B. Burke (S.A.)	11.7
1950 S.B. Strickland (Aus.)	11.6
1954 E.M. Maskell (N. Rhod.)	10.9
1958 N.C. Thrower (Aus.)	10.7
1962 P. Kilborn (Aus.)	10.9
1966 P. Kilborn (Aus.)	10.9

100 metres hurdles	sec.
1970 P. Kilborn (Aus.)	13.2
1974 J.A. Vernon (Eng.)	13.45
1978 L.M. Boothe (Eng.)	12.98
1982 S. Strong (Eng.)	12.78

110 × 220 × 110 yards relay | sec.
1934 England | 49.4
1938 Australia | 49.1
1950 Australia | 47.9

4 × 110 yards relay | sec.
1954 Australia | 46.8
1958 England | 45.3
1962 Australia | 46.6
1966 Australia | 45.3

4 × 100 metres relay | sec.
1970 Australia | 44.1
1974 Australia | 43.51
1978 England | 43.70
1982 England | 43.15

660 yards relay | min. sec.
1934 Canada | 1 14.4
1938 Australia | 1 15.2
1950 Australia | 1 13.4

4 × 400 metres relay | min. sec.
1974 England | 3 29.2
1978 England | 3 27.2
1982 Canada | 3 27.8

High jump | metres
1934 M.R. Clark (S.A.) | 1.60
1938 D.J.B. Tyler (Eng.) | 1.60
1950 D.J.B. Tyler (Eng.) | 1.60
1954 T.E. Hopkins (N. Ire.) | 1.67
1958 M.M. Mason (Aus.) | 1.70
1962 R. Woodhouse (Aus.) | 1.78
1966 M.M. Brown (Aus.)* | 1.72
1970 D. Brill (Canada) | 1.78
1974 B.J. Lawton (Eng.) | 1.84
1978 K. Gibbs (Aus.) | 1.93
1982 D. Brill (Canada) | 1.88
*née Mason

Long jump | metres
1934 P. Bartholomew (Eng.) | 5.47
1938 D. Norman (Aus.) | 5.80
1950 Y.W. Williams (N.Z.) | 5.90
1954 Y.W. Williams (N.Z.) | 6.08
1958 S.H. Hoskins (Eng.) | 6.02
1962 P. Kilborn (Aus.) | 6.27
1966 M.D. Rand (Eng.) | 6.36
1970 S. Sherwood (Eng.) | 6.73
1974 M. Oshikoya (Nigeria) | 6.46
1978 S.D. Reeve (Eng.) | 6.59
1982 S. Ferguson (Bahamas) | 6.91

Shot | metres
1954 Y.W. Williams (N.Z.) | 13.96
1958 V.I. Sloper (N.Z.) | 15.54
1962 V.I. Young (N.Z.)* | 15.23
1966 V.I. Young (N.Z.) | 16.50
1970 M.E. Peters (N. Ire.) | 15.93
1974 J. Haist (Canada) | 16.12
1978 G. Mulhall (Aus.) | 17.31
1982 J. Oakes (Eng.) | 17.92
*née Sloper

Discus | metres
1954 Y.W. Williams (N.Z.) | 45.02
1958 S. Allday (Eng.) | 45.90
1962 V.I. Young (N.Z.) | 50.20
1966 V.I. Young (N.Z.) | 49.78
1970 C.R. Payne (Scot.) | 54.46
1974 J. Haist (Canada) | 55.52
1978 C. Ionescu (Canada) | 62.16
1982 M. Ritchie (Scot.) | 62.98

Javelin | metres
1934 G.A. Lunn (Eng.) | 32.18
1938 R. Higgins (Canada) | 38.28
1950 C.C. McGibbon (Aus.) | 38.84
1954 M.C. Swanepoel (S.A.) | 43.82
1958 A. Pazera (Aus.) | 57.40
1962 S. Platt (Eng.) | 50.24
1966 M. Parker (Aus.) | 51.38
1970 P. Rivers (Aus.) | 52.00
1974 P. Rivers (Aus.) | 55.48
1978 T.I. Sanderson (Eng.) | 61.34
1982 S. Howland (Aus.) | 64.46

Pentathlon | points
1970 M.E. Peters (N. Ire.) | 4524
1974 M.E. Peters (N. Ire.) | 4455
1978 D. Konihowski (Canada) | 4768

Heptathlon | points
1982 G. Nunn (Aus.) | 6282

World Championships
Helsinki, 1983
Gold, silver and bronze medallists
Men's events

100 metres | sec.
1. C. Lewis (USA) | 10.07
2. C. Smith (USA) | 10.21
3. E. King (USA) | 10.24

200 metres   sec.
1. C. Smith (USA)   20.14
2. E. Quow (USA)   20.41
3. P. Menna (Italy)   20.51

400 metres   sec.
1. B. Cameron (Jam.)   45.05
2. M. Franks (USA)   45.22
3. S. Nix (USA)   45.24

800 metres   min. sec.
1. W. Wulbeck (FRG)   1 43.65
2. R. Druppers (Neth.)   1 44.20
3. J. Cruz (Brazil)   1 44.27

1500 metres   min. sec.
1. S. Cram (GB)   3 41.59
2. S. Scott (USA)   3 41.87
3. S. Aouita (Morocco)   3 42.02

5000 metres   min. sec.
1. E. Coghlan (Ireland)   13 28.53
2. W. Schildhauer (GDR)   13 30.20
3. M. Vainio (Fin.)   13 30.34

10,000 metres   min. sec.
1. A. Cova (Italy)   28 01.04
2. W. Schildhauer (GDR)   28 01.18
3. H. Kunze (GDR)   28 01.26

Marathon   h. min. sec.
1. R. de Castella (Aus.)   2 10 03.00
2. K. Balcha (Eth.)   2 10 27.00
3. W. Cierpinski (GDR)   2 10 37.00

3000 metres steeplechase   min. sec.
1. P. Ilg (FRG)   8 15.06
2. B. Maminski (Pol.)   8 17.03
3. C. Reitz (GB)   8 17.75

110 metres hurdles   sec.
1. G. Foster (USA)   13.42
2. A. Bryggare (Fin.)   13.46
3. W. Gault (USA)   13.48

400 metres hurdles   sec.
1. E. Moses (USA)   47.50
2. H. Schmid (FRG)   48.61
3. A. Kharlov (USSR)   49.03

High jump   metres
1. G. Avdeyenko (USSR)   2.32
2. T. Peacock (USA)   2.32
3. Z. Jian Hua (China)   2.29

Pole vault   metres
1. S. Bubka (USSR)   5.70
2. K. Volkov (USSR)   5.60
3. A. Tarev (Bulg.)   5.60

Long jump   metres
1. C. Lewis (USA)   8.55
2. J. Grimes (USA)   8.29
3. M. Conley (USA)   8.12

Triple jump   metres
1. Z. Hoffman (Pol.)   17.42
2. W. Banks (USA)   17.18
3. A. Agbebaku (Nigeria)   17.18

Shot put   metres
1. E. Sarul (Pol.)   21.39
2. U. Timmermann (GDR)   21.16
3. R. Machura (Czech.)   20.98

Discus   metres
1. I. Bugar (Czech.)   67.22
2. L. Delis (Cuba)   67.36
3. G. Valent (Czech.)   66.08

Hammer   metres
1. S. Litvinov (USSR)   82.68
2. Y. Sedykh (USSR)   80.94
3. Z. Kwasny (Pol.)   79.42

Javelin   metres
1. D. Michel (GDR)   89.48
2. T. Petranoff (USA)   85.60
3. D. Kula (USSR)   85.58

Decathlon   points
1. F.M. Thompson (GB)   8666
2. J. Hingsen (FRG)   8561
3. S. Wentz (FRG)   8478

4 × 100 metres relay   sec.
1. United States   37.86
2. Italy   38.37
3. USSR   38.41

4 × 400 metres relay   min. sec.
1. USSR   3 00.79
2. West Germany   3 01.83
3. Great Britain   3 03.53

20 kilometres walk   h. min. sec.
1. E. Canto (Mexico)   1 20 49.00

| 2. J. Pribilinec (Czech.) | 1 20 59.00 |
| 3. Y. Yevsyukov (USSR) | 1 21 08.00 |

50 kilometres walk   h. min. sec.
1. R. Weigel (GDR)	3 43 08.00
2. J. Marin (Spain)	3 46 42.00
3. S. Jung (USSR)	3 49 03.00

Women's events

100 metres   sec.
1. M. Gohr (GDR)	10.97
2. M. Koch (GDR)	11.02
3. D. Williams (USA)	11.06

200 metres   sec.
1. M. Koch (GDR)	22.13
2. M. Ottey (Jam.)	22.19
3. K. Cook (GB)	22.37

400 metres   sec.
1. J. Kratochvilova (Czech.)	47.99
2. T. Kocembova (Czech.)	48.59
3. M. Pinigina (USSR)	49.19

800 metres   min. sec.
1. J. Kratochvilova (Czech.)	1 54.68
2. L. Gurina (USSR)	1 56.11
3. Y. Podkopayeva (USSR)	1 57.58

1500 metres   min. sec.
1. M. Decker (USA)	4 00.90
2. Z. Zaitseva (USSR)	4 01.19
3. Y. Podkopayeva (USSR)	4 02.25

3000 metres   min. sec.
1. M. Decker (USA)	8 34.62
2. B. Kraus (FRG)	8 35.11
3. T. Kazankina (USSR)	8 35.13

Marathon   h. min. sec.
1. G. Waitz (Norway)	2 28 09.00
2. M. Dickerson (USA)	2 31 09.00
3. R. Smekhnova (USSR)	2 31 13.00

100 metres hurdles   sec.
| 1. B. Jahn (GDR) | 12.35 |

| 2. K. Knabe (GDR) | 12.42 |
| 3. G. Zagorcheva (Bulg.) | 12.62 |

400 metres hurdles   sec.
1. Y. Fesenko (USSR)	54.14
2. A. Ambrozene (USSR)	54.15
3. E. Fiedler (GDR)	54.55

High jump   metres
1. T. Bykova (USSR)	2.01
2. U. Meyfarth (FRG)	1.99
3. L. Ritter (USA)	1.95

Long jump   metres
1. H. Daute (GDR)	7.27
2. A. Cusmir (Romania)	7.15
3. C. Lewis (USA)	7.04

Shot   metres
1. H. Fibingerova (Czech.)	21.05
2. H. Knorscheidt (GDR)	20.70
3. I. Slupianek (GDR)	20.56

Discus   metres
1. M. Opitz (GDR)	68.94
2. G. Murashova (USSR)	67.44
3. M. Petkova (Bulg.)	66.44

Javelin   metres
1. T. Lillak (Fin.)	70.82
2. F. Whitbread (GB)	69.14
3. A. Verouli (Greece)	65.72

Heptathlon   points
1. R. Neubert (GDR)	6714
2. S. Paetz (GDR)	6662
3. A. Vater (GDR)	6532

4 × 100 metres relay   sec.
1. GDR	41.76
2. Great Britain	42.71
3. Jamaica	42.73

4 × 400 metres relay   min. sec.
1. GDR	3 19.73
2. Czechoslovakia	3 20.32
3. USSR	3 21.16

Athletics record performances as at 31 December 1983

Categories: World (W); European (E); Commonwealth (C); UK National (UK)

len's events

Event	Cat.	Time/Dist.	Athlete	Venue	Date
)0 m	W	9.93	Calvin Smith (USA)	Colorado Springs	3.7.83
	C	10.04	Lennox Miller (JAM)	Mexico City	14.10.68
	E	10.01	Pietro Mennea (ITA)	Mexico City	4.9.79
	UK	10.11	Alan Wells (UK)	Moscow	24.7.80
)0 m	W,E	19.72	Pietro Mennea (ITA)	Mexico City	12.9.79
	C	19.86	Don Quarrie (JAM)	Cali	3.8.71
	UK	20.21	Alan Wells (UK)	Moscow	28.7.80
)0 m	W	43.86	Lee Evans (USA)	Mexico City	18.10.68
	E	44.50	Erwin Skamrahl (FRG)	Munich	26.7.83
	C	44.58	Bert Cameron (JAM)	Baton Rouge	6.6.81
	UK	44.93	Dave Jenkins (UK)	Eugene	21.6.75
0 m	W,E,C,UK	1:41.73	Sebastian Coe (UK)	Florence	10.6.81
00 m	W,E,C,UK	2:12.18	Sebastian Coe (UK)	Oslo	11.7.81
00 m	W,E,C,UK	3:30.77	Steve Ovett (UK)	Rieti	4.9.83
ile	W,E,C,UK	3:47.33	Sebastian Coe (UK)	Brussels	28.8.81
00 m	W,C	4:51.4	John Walker (NZ)	Oslo	30.6.76
	E	4:52.20	Thomas Wessinghage (FRG)	Ingleheim	31.8.82
	UK	4:57.71	Steve Ovett (UK)	Oslo	7.7.82
00 m	W,C	7:32.1	Henry Rono (KEN)	Oslo	27.6.78
	E,UK	7:32.79	David Moorcroft (UK)	London	17.7.82
00 m	W,E,C,UK	13:00.41	David Moorcroft (UK)	Oslo	7.7.82
km	W,C	27:22.4	Henry Rono (KEN)	Vienna	11.6.78
	E	27:22.95	Fernando Mamede (POR)	Paris	9.7.82
	UK	27:30.3	Brendan Foster (UK)	London	23.6.78
km	W,E	57:24.2	Jos Hermens (NETH)	Papendal	1.5.76
	C	58:37.2	Rob De Castella (AUS)	Rome	17.4.82
	UK	58:39.0	Ron Hill (UK)	Leicester	9.11.68
hour	W,E	20,944 m	Jos Hermens (NETH)	Papendal	1.5.76
	C	20,516	Rob De Castella (AUS)	Rome	17.4.82
	UK	20,472	Ron Hill (UK)	Leicester	9.11.68
km	W	1:13:55.8	Toshihiko Seko (JAP)	Christchurch, NZ	22.3.81
	E	1:14:16.8	Pekka Paivarinta (FIN)	Oulu	15.5.75
	C,UK	1:15:22.6	Ron Hill (UK)	Bolton	21.7.65
km	W	1:29:18.8	Toshihiko Seko (JAP)	Christchurch, NZ	22.3.81
	E,C,UK	1:31:30.4	Jim Alder (UK)	London	5.9.70
0 m H	W	12.93	Renaldo Nehemiah (USA)	Zurich	19.8.81
	E	13.28	Guy Drut (FRA)	St Etienne	29.6.75
	C	13.37	Mark McKoy (CAN)	Brisbane	4.10.82
	UK	13.43	Mark Holtom (UK)	Brisbane	4.10.82
0 m H	W	47.02	Ed Moses (USA)	Koblenz	31.8.83
	E	47.48	Harald Schmid (FRG)	Athens	8.9.82
	C	47.82	John Akii-Bua (UGA)	Munich	2.9.72
	UK	48.12	David Hemery (UK)	Mexico City	15.10.68
00 m SC	W,C	8:05.4	Henry Rono (KEN)	Seattle	13.5.78
	E	8:08.02	Anders Garderud (SWE)	Montreal	28.7.76
	UK	8:15.16	Graeme Fell (UK)	West Berlin	17.8.83
100 m R	W	37.86	USA	Helsinki	10.8.83
	E	38.26	USSR	Moscow	1.8.80

Event		Time/Dist	Name	Place	Date
	C	38.39	Jamaica	Mexico City	19.10.6
	UK	38.62	UK National Team	Moscow	1.8.8
4 × 200 m R	W	1:20.26	Univ. of Southern California	Tempe	27.5.7
	E	1:21.5	Italy	Barletta	21.7.7.
	C	1:22.5	Trinidad & Tobago	Barletta	21.7.7.
	UK	1:24.1	UK National Team	Paris	2.10.7
4 × 400 m R	W	2:56.16	USA	Mexico City	20.10.6
	C	2:59.64	Kenya	Mexico City	20.10.6
	E,UK	3:00.46	UK National Team	Munich	10.9.7
4 × 800 m R	W,E,C,UK	7:03.89	UK National Team	London	30.8.8.
4 × 1500 m R	W,E	14:38.8	FRG	Cologne	17.8.7
	C	14:40.4	New Zealand	Oslo	22.8.7
	UK	14:56.8	UK National Team	Bourges	23.6.7.
Road walking					
20 km walk*	W	1:18:49	Daniel Bautista (MEX)	Eschborn	29.9.7
	E	1:19:11	Gennadiy Terekhov (USSR)	Russe	13.4.8
	C	1:20:51	David Smith (AUS)	Luxembourg	21.8.8
	UK	1:22:51	Steve Barry (UK)	Douglas, IOM	26.2.8
30 km walk*	W	2:03:06	Daniel Bautista (MEX)	Cherkassy	27.4.8
	E	2:05:05	Pyotr Pochenchuk (USSR)	Cherkassy	27.4.8
	C	2:08:01	Willi Sawall (AUS)	Melbourne	16.5.82
	UK	2:10:16	Steve Barry (UK)	Brisbane	7.10.82
50 km walk*	W,E	3:37:36	Yevhen Ivchenko (USSR)	Moscow	24.5.80
	C	3:46:34	Willi Sawall (AUS)	Adelaide	6.4.80
	UK	4:02:38	Chris Maddocks (UK)	Bergen	24.9.83
Track Walking					
2 hour walk	W,E	28,165 m	Jose Marin (SPA)	Barcelona	8.4.79
	C	27,123 m	Willi Sawall (AUS)	Box Hill	24.5.80
	UK	26,037 m	Ron Wallwork (UK)	Stretford	21.7.71
High jump	W	2.37 m	Zhu Jian Hua (CHI)	Shanghai	22.9.83
	E	2.36	Gerd Wessig (GDR)	Moscow	1.8.80
	C	2.32	Milt Ottey (JAM)	Provo	4.6.82
	UK	2.25	Geoff Parsons (UK)	Plymouth	9.7.83
Long jump	W	8.90 m	Bob Beamon (USA)	Mexico City	18.10.68
	E	8.54	Lutz Dombrowski (GDR)	Moscow	28.7.70
	C,UK	8.13	Lynn Davies (UK)	Berne	30.6.68
Pole vault	W,E	5.83 m	Thierry Vigneron (FRA)	Rome	1.9.83
	C,UK	5.65	Keith Stock (UK)	Stockholm	7.7.81
Triple jump	W	17.89 m	Joao Carlos De Oliviera (BRA)	Mexico City	15.10.75
	E,C,UK	17.57	Keith Connor (UK)	Provo	5.6.82
Shot put	W,E	22.22 m	Udo Beyer (GDR)	Los Angeles	25.6.83
	C,UK	21.68	Geoff Capes (UK)	Cwmbran	18.5.80
Discus	W,E	71.86 m	Yuriy Dumchev (USSR)	Moscow	29.5.83
	C	66.72	Brad Cooper (BAH)	Havana	8.8.82
	UK	64.32	Bill Tancred (UK)	Woodford	10.8.74
Hammer	W,E	84.14 m	Sergey Litvinov (USSR)	Moscow	21.6.83
	C	75.90	Peter Farmer (AUS)	Vanves	14.8.79
	UK	75.40	Chris Black (UK)	London	23.7.83
Javelin	W	99.72 m	Tom Petranoff (USA)	Westwood	15.5.83
	E	96.72	Ferenc Paragi (HUN)	Tata	23.4.80
			Detlef Michel (GDR)	Berlin	8.6.83

* There are no official world records for road walking but the performances listed are generally accepted as the world's best authentic performances.

Event		Mark	Athlete	Location	Date
	C	90.58	Mike O'Rourke (AUS)	Aukland	23.1.83
	UK	85.52	Dave Ottley (UK)	Isleworth	28.5.80
Decathlon	W,E	8777	Jurgen Hingsen (FRG)	Bernhausen	5.6.83
	C,UK	8743	F.M. Thompson (UK)	Athens	8.9.82

Women's events

Event		Mark	Athlete	Location	Date
100 m	W	10.79	Evelyn Ashford (USA)	Colorado Springs	3.7.83
	E	10.81	Marlies Gohr (GDR)	Berlin	8.6.83
	C	11.00	Angela Taylor (CAN)	Brisbane	4.10.82
	UK	11.10	Kathy Smallwood (UK)	Rome	5.9.81
200 m	W,E	21.71	Marita Koch (GDR)	Karl-Marx-Stadt	10.6.79
	C,UK	22.13	Kathy Smallwood (UK)	Athens	9.9.82
400 m	W,E	47.99	Jarmila Kratochvilova (CZE)	Helsinki	10.8.83
	C	50.06	Marita Payne (CAN)	Helsinki	10.8.83
	UK	50.46	Kathy Cook (UK)	London	17.9.82
800 m	W,E	1:53.28	Jarmila Kratochvilova (CZE)	Munich	26.7.83
	C	1:59.0	Charlene Rendina (AUS)	Melbourne	28.2.76
	UK	1:59.05	Christina Boxer (UK)	Turin	4.8.79
1500 m	W,E	3:52.47	Tatyana Kazankina (USSR)	Zurich	13.8.80
	C,UK	4:01.53	Chris Benning (UK)	Zurich	15.8.79
3000 m	W,E	8:26.78	Svetlana Ulmasova (USSR)	Kiev	25.7.82
	C,UK	8:37.06	Wendy Sly (UK)	Helsinki	10.8.83
5000 m	W	15:08.26	Mary Decker (USA)	Eugene	5.6.82
	E	15:08.80	Grete Waitz (NOR)	Oslo	26.6.82
	C	15:13.22	Anne Audain (NZ)	Auckland	17.3.82
	UK	14:54.51	Paula Fudge (UK)	Knarvik	13.9.81
10 km	W,E	31:27.57	Raisa Sadretdinova (USSR)	Odessa	7.9.83
	C,UK	32:57.17	Kathy Binns (UK)	Sittard	14.8.80
Mile	W,E	4:17.44	Maricica Puica (ROM)	Rieti	16.9.82
	C	4:29.67	Debbie Scott (CAN)	Oslo	26.6.82
	UK	4:30.20	Christina Boxer (UK)	Gateshead	8.7.79
100 m H	W,E	12.36	Grazyna Rabstyn (POL)	Warsaw	13.6.80
	C,UK	12.87	Shirley Strong (UK)	Zurich	24.8.83
400 m H	W,E	54.02	Anna Ambrozene (USSR)	Moscow	11.6.83
	C	55.89	Debbie Flintoff (AUS)	Brisbane	7.10.82
	UK	56.04	Sue Morley (UK)	Helsinki	10.8.83
5 km walk	W,E	22:14.01	Alexandra Derevinskaya (USSR)	Oryol	11.7.82
	C	22:32.4	Sue Cook (AUS)	Sydney	22.5.82
	UK	23:11.2	Carol Tyson (UK)	Ostersund	30.6.79
10 km walk	W,C	46:42.6	Sue Cook (AUS)	Adelaide	23.5.82
	E	47:49.3	Ann Jansson (SWE)	Vasteras	19.6.82
	UK	48:11.0	Marion Fawkes (UK)	Gunnisfalt	8.7.79
4 × 100 m R	W,E	41.53	GDR	Berlin	31.7.83
	C,UK	42.43	UK National Team	Moscow	1.8.80
4 × 200 m R	W,E	1:28.15	GDR	Jena	9.8.80
	C,UK	1:31.57	UK National Team	London	20.8.77
4 × 400 m R	W,E	3:19.04	GDR	Athens	11.9.82
	C	3:25.26	Canada	Edmonton	9.7.83
	UK	3:25.82	UK National Team	Athens	11.9.82
4 × 800 m R	W,E	7:52.3	USSR	Podolsk	16.8.76
	C,UK	8:23.8	UK National Team	Paris	2.10.71

Event		Mark	Athlete	Venue	Date
High jump	W,E	2.04 m	Tamara Bykova (USSR)	Pisa	25.8.8
	C	1.97	Debbie Brill (CAN)	Berne	19.7.8
	UK	1.95	Diana Elliott (UK)	Oslo	26.6.8
Long jump	W,E	7.43 m	Anisoara Cusmir (ROM)	Bucharest	5.6.8
	C,UK	6.90	Beverley Kinch (UK)	Helsinki	14.8.8
Shot put	W,E	22.45 m	Ilona Slupianek (GDR)	Potsdam	11.5.8
	C,UK	18.99	Meg Ritchie (UK)	Tucson	7.5.8
Discus	W,E	73.26 m	Galina Savinkova (USSR)	Leselidse	22.5.8
	C,UK	67.48	Meg Ritchie (UK)	Walnut	26.4.8
Javelin	W,E	74.76 m	Tina Lillak (FIN)	Tampere	13.6.8
	C,UK	73.58	Tessa Sanderson (UK)	Edinburgh	26.6.8
Heptathlon	W,E	6836	Ramona Neubert (GDR)	Moscow	19.6.8
	C,UK	6353	Judy Livermore (UK)	Sofia	12.9.8